DEDICATION

I would like to dedicate this book to my late grandmother, *Ida Hardy.* Your words live on through me, and I will never forget the life lessons you gave me directly and indirectly through the way you lived your life. Your life was exemplary of service to others, always thinking of others first. I aspire to live my life in such a manner. Grandma, you set a precedent of what life should be: how our very existence is never just for us, but to enhance the lives of others in a positive way through sharing our God-given gifts.

I know you're looking down on me from the heavens, and I will do everything in my power to continue to make you proud. This book and every one from here on out is dedicated to you and the lasting legacy you've left in the lives of so many. I miss you and love you.

Your grandson,

Matthew

CONTENTS

PREFACE

Do questions such as "What is my purpose in life?" and "What is my *IT*?" seem to find their way into your thoughts? With so many people out there lacking any purpose, I felt the need to provide people with hope and direction for their future. I believe that there are no accidents or coincidences in life, and that the dream that resides inside of you is strategically placed by the all-knowing Creator, God, who entrusted you with His precious plan for your life. In this book, I will provide you with the tools that will let you gain an awareness of the brilliance, genius, and greatness that everyone possesses, but few rarely connect to.

You have my unending promise that after reading this book, you'll never view yourself in the same light. You'll know in the core of your being that you were born to surpass any limitations or obstacles that appear in your path, and evolve into divine greatness.

Regardless of your past successes or failures, your best days are in front of you. This is why my company motto states "Your Best Life Possible Awaits You." Allow me, through the words on these pages, to walk you to the doorstep of Your Best Life Possible by connecting you to your God-given dream and destiny. May you know that your dream is truly *the pathway* to discovering your true existence and becoming everything your Creator has predestined you to become.

THE DREAM

Dᴿᴇᴀᴍˢ ᴏʀ ᴅᴇˢɪʀᴇˢ ᴅᴏɴ’ᴛ ᴊᴜˢᴛ ᴀᴘᴘᴇᴀʀ ɪɴ ʏᴏᴜʀ ʜᴇᴀʀᴛ, ᴛʜᴇʏ ʜᴀᴠᴇ ᴘᴜʀ-
ᴘᴏˢᴇ ʙᴇʜɪɴᴅ ᴛʜᴇᴍ ᴀɴᴅ ᴀʀᴇ ᴅᴇˢɪɢɴᴇᴅ ʙʏ ᴛʜᴇ Cʀᴇᴀᴛᴏʀ ᴛᴏ ʙᴇ ᴘᴜʀˢᴜᴇᴅ
ғᴏʀ ᴀɴ ᴏᴜᴛᴄᴏᴍᴇ ᴏɴʟʏ Hᴇ ᴋɴᴏᴡˢ ᴏғ. MATTHEW C. HORNE

Recognizing the dream in your heart and submitting to it is the first and most pivotal step to entering The Creator's infinite universe and experiencing a life filled with amenities you only dreamed of! Just think for a second...of all the different routes you could have taken in life, all of the different things you could become in this grand universe. Why is your heart pulling you in a specific direction? These are the types of questions great people ask themselves on a continual basis. I say continual because your heart is always pulling you in a direction that supersedes your current standing.

These are the questions that will pull you out of your nine-to-five life and walk you into your place within the universe. That dream in your heart is there for a reason. The desires you have that don't go away, despite circumstances that should have drowned them out by now, are still there because they are actually an extension of the Creator who saw fit for you to exist in this world. Your dream is your best output possible that you can give to this world. It is the best because your Creator is the only infallible existence there is. If He put an extension of Himself in you, then it is a sure-fire plan for you to carry out something He has intended for you to do, a plan made before you arrived here in this earthly realm. I hope that you can now begin to see that your dream isn't just another part of you, but the result of strategic placement by your Creator.

——➤◦◄——

Separate Your Dream from You

Your dream is an extension of God that resides in you. Once you really grasp that fact, then hesitancy will no longer exist, because you'll know that if your dream is something that is an extension of God, and not something your fallible self has manufactured for you, then the doubt will subside, and contemplation of the perfect nature of this dream will replace what was once doubtful thinking. If you put your faith in man or yourself, you'll be disappointed in some capacity every time; but if you put your faith in God, He'll do anything but fail.

Taking steps in the direction of your dream means putting absolute faith in your Creator. The way God designed it is that everyone has some sort of dream or desire they want to fulfill in life, and if you don't, you're just not looking within yourself hard enough! With the placement of this dream comes doubt and uncertainty concerning whether you can achieve it or not. This uncertainty is also the result of strategic placement. If you could just actualize your dream without internal or external opposition, there would be no need for you to have faith.

It is boldly stated in your Creator's Success Manual—known as the Bible—that "without faith it is impossible to please Him." With that being said, it's part of the Creator's plan that you will have to continually overcome doubt and opposition in the pursuit of your dream. Activating your dream is the initial act of faith that puts you in the ball game and sets you on your course to actualizing your dream! From start to finish, there is nothing you can do to make yourself deserving of having your dreams come to pass. The qualifier is simply having the faith to face the obstacles you'll encounter, and believing that your Creator will see you through all of the rough spots, in spite of what your natural situation or circumstance indicates. For without faith, it is impossible for your Creator to advance you to your next step in your dream pursuit.

According to Robert T. Kiyosaki, author of the *Rich Dad, Poor Dad* series, "Five percent of the world's cash flow is generated by 95 percent of the world's working-class population. Ninety-five percent of the world's cash flow is generated by business owners who only comprise 5 percent of the population." All cash flow is a derivative of someone's dream. Your lifetime earnings are dependent upon whether you'll support someone else's dream, or step into that 5th percentile who generate 95 percent of the world's income—those who just dared to believe in their dream!

When you make a conscious decision to follow your dream, you've done what the majority of society won't do! You're not on your way to success or failure, rather truth. As human beings, we'll always have a desire to surpass our current condition, because we are ever-evolving beings. There will be unrest within you, regardless of how much success or wealth you have attained, if you aren't exerting yourself in a way that facilitates your achieving more in life.

———◆———

The Truth of Your Dream

The dream that's in your heart may not necessarily be your IT in life, it may just be meant to put you in the vicinity of your true IT!

On life's journey, you will find that some things you envisioned yourself becoming represented the truth of who you are, because you actualized what was once a dream. Dreams that facilitate success in the arena in which they place you are truth. Some of the conceptions you have for yourself at the beginning of dream pursuit do not always materialize themselves. This isn't a bad thing, because any desire that's in your heart that you pursue until the end will actualize itself, or put you in the vicinity of some intricate part of yourself that the Creator knew you had all along that is absolutely pivotal to fulfilling your destiny.

Let me share my experience with you. I entered Coastal Carolina University in Conway, South Carolina, as an athletic, 6 feet 5 inches tall, lights-out shooter. I had a dream of becoming an NBA player. Given my physical attributes, this wasn't unrealistic. In the second semester of my sophomore year, I took a speech class that turned out to be life-changing. My teacher, Mr. Jones, assigned everyone in the class to give a persuasive speech. He went around the class and allowed everyone to state the topic of the speeches they would present. When he got to me, before I could even open my mouth, he said, "And Matthew, he's going to do basketball." I thought to myself, "I didn't get to pick my speech topic yet, and still I want to help everyone in the class." The night before I was to give my speech, I put a presentation together entitled "Continued Success in the Game of Basketball." I may have rehearsed it one time. I really didn't put much effort into it.

So there I was the next day, in front of my classmates with a table displaying a jersey from every era of basketball I'd ever participated in, from the Boys and Girls Club all the way to NCAA Division I Coastal Carolina. I even had the audacity to place a pair of authentic NBA basketball shorts beside my Coastal Carolina jersey to signify that I would get drafted when it was all said and done.

After setting everything up, I told the class the title of my speech and began the presentation. I talked about playing at the Boys and Girls Club and how I had a vision to make my middle-school team while I was playing at that level. I then moved to my middle-school jersey and shocked my classmates by throwing my Boys and Girls Club jersey at them. My reasoning was that the jersey didn't exist anymore, because in order to achieve success in life, you must look forward and not look back. I then went from my middle-school jersey to my high-school jersey. Once again, I threw my middle-school jersey at them, signifying that I was looking forward to my Division I hoop dreams and not looking backward. I then went from my high-school jersey to my Division I Coastal Carolina jersey. There I was, giving a speech in my sophomore year, with two years of eligibility left, at a university where my playing time was scarce at best, and I had the faith to throw a Coastal Carolina jersey at my classmates, to once again emphasize the fact that you must look forward in order to continually succeed in life. All that remained on that table was the pair of NBA shorts, because I believed I was going to the NBA, I just didn't know which team I would play for.

I then urged my classmates to believe that they had the same capabilities to achieve continued success if they would look forward and not backward in life. After I finished giving my speech, I received an overwhelming response. Later, five of my classmates pulled me to the side, and told me with the most genuine looks of sincerity I've ever seen that I should be a motivational speaker. I laughed it off and thought they were joking. I nonchalantly snickered, and said, "I'm six foot five with a jump shot.... Motivational speaker? Are you kidding me?" But as I said that, the sincere look on their faces didn't change.

I had a dream of becoming an NBA player, which I can say in retrospect was there for a reason. It didn't actualize itself, but it revealed a truth about me that was undeniably the key to my fulfilling my destiny. Don't be disappointed when things don't go the way you had envisioned at the onset of your dream pursuit, because I'll guarantee you that if you see your dreams through until the end, you will have emerged into the very thing the Creator knew you were before the foundation of this world. Truth is the only lasting element at the end of dream pursuit, not success or failure. That's why I say with confidence that you must pursue the dream that is in your heart, because dreams are the pathway to your discovering your true existence and becoming everything the Creator has intended for you to become. When you're everything your Creator already knows you are, it is then, and only then, that you can live life at its optimum. I say this because you are incapable of manufacturing a plan for your life that could ever rival that of the one the Creator has laid out for you.

The Success Manual clearly states that "there is a way that seemeth right to a man, but the end thereof is death." This isn't a physical death, so to speak, but a death that will qualify you as a walking corpse. When you step outside of your predestined genetic makeup and attempt to find success there, it is never whole. The Creator's path is laid out in such a way that not only will you have the financial amenities that qualify you as a "success," but you will also have the inner peace that can only be attributed to occupying your designed space within the universe.

I know everyone has been exposed to someone who seemingly has it all: the house, the cars, the luxuries that our society defines as success, but when you look at their everyday actions and demeanor, you can tell something is missing. Yes, something is missing: the internal peace and soundness of mind that comes along with submitting to THE PLAN for your life; and not manufacturing "a plan" and calling it success when it becomes reality. I heard a wise man say something that kept me in the game many times when I wanted to fold my hand and attain my dreams my way. He said, "The most evil thing you could do is knowingly walk away from the will of God for your life." He then said, "Evil manifests itself in the end." People think they can create a plan that's better than the one the Creator has laid out for them, but if and when they actually attain it, they see that there is something missing, which is then conveyed to us with a look of despair in the midst of what society defines as "a lavish lifestyle."

The universe is always giving you signs that point you in the direction of your space within it. The sole objective for our Creation is that we occupy our space within this universe we exist in. Following that dream in your heart may appear to you, and others around you, as if you are taking steps backward, but in all actuality you are taking gargantuan leaps in the direction of your space within the universe... leaps in the direction of your best life possible!

If there's still any question about anything I've said within this chapter, just look at the Academy Awards show and listen to the speech pattern of all the Oscar recipients when they step on stage, tears streaming down their face: "It all started with a dream...."; "I was just a....!" If you follow your dream and uncompromisingly see it through, your speech, too, will sound something like theirs.

—————————

The Dream

Abandoned by many
Yet given to all
Never scraping our potential's surface
Is this creation's downfall

The dream
Actualized in an instant
No respecter of persons
Even to society's misfits

If seen through to completion
Its possibilities prove infinite
If an about-face isn't performed
When life's weather gets inclement

What you see so vividly
Others so hastily disagree
There's no truth to it
Opinionated words from their philosophy

If they haven't done it

What makes them think you can

It's an intrinsic knowing

That will guide you to your plan

So hold fast to it

As if it's life or death

Get in the theater of your mind

And you'll see its height and its depth

Stay the course

And its depictions will become more vivid

What was once a dream

In its midst you will stand as you live it

Notes and Insights

THE STRUGGLE

The struggle, the wall, a reversal of fortune, whatever you want to call it—but call it inevitable, because any person who has achieved greatness in life can attest to the fact that the struggle is something they've encountered on their way to the top, and it's something that remains until this very day. Oh, but don't be discouraged when you reach the struggle, because this is where your greatness comes to the forefront, and your legacy, the permeating thought that lives beyond you in the minds of others, is solidified.

The struggle occurs when you've set your dreams in motion and everything is seemingly going well for you. All of a sudden, anything and everything that could possibly go wrong does. You say things to yourself like, "What did I do to deserve this? I'm an upstanding person. I go to church," and more familiar phrases that validate us as not having to go through the struggle. But, everyone deserves the struggle.

Everyone deserves to overcome the obstacles that life sets before them, so they can truly discover their inner genius and greatness.

When I was playing basketball in college, I never logged significant minutes on the court, but I was one of the hardest-working players on the team. I was in the gym so much, it was as if it were my second job. I improved tremendously as a player, just not in a way that my coach envisioned would allow me to play in his offense. I increased my workload every year in spite of my lack of playing time. It's as if the harder I worked, the worse my circumstances became in the pursuit of my hoop dreams: but still, I totally immersed myself in the vision I had in my heart of becoming a professional basketball player. I somehow found the inner drive to wake up every morning during the summer and go to the gym for at least an hour and a half of drills that my coach had designed for me at the end of each season.

When I came back to school after every summer, drastic improvements in my game and physique were evident. It was an indescribable struggle to go through this rigorous training regimen every summer, yet still find myself in the same position I was in during the previous year. After a while, I knew I had done everything physically possible to improve as a basketball player, and I began to ask myself questions like, "What did I do to deserve this? I know I have the talent. Why did my coach even recruit me?"

One day during my junior year of college, I happened to be watching Bishop T. D. Jakes on television and heard him say, "When you can't change your situation, just change your perspective." In that one moment I gained an awareness of the greatness that the Creator was extracting from my inner being during my struggle, and I changed my perspective in the midst of the uncommonly adverse situation I was in at the time. When my perspective changed, I could see myself emerging into a motivational speaker.

*Emergence **always** takes place in the midst of dream pursuit; not necessarily in the fashion you'd like, but rather in the fashion it's designed to.*

I could see at that very moment, during Bishop T. D. Jakes' telecast, that my being at Coastal Carolina University, not cracking the lineup, but rather being in that speech class during my sophomore year with everyone eagerly trying to persuade me to be a motivational speaker, was just one huge setup. I really changed my point of view from woe-is-me to what-is-this-doing-for-me. When this happened, it was as if blinders were taken off my eyes and the Creator gave me a glimpse of what this trying time in my life was all about. I was emerging into a motivational speaker, and the reason I thought I was at Coastal Carolina University wasn't the real reason at all. I was in the vicinity of everything I needed in order to become a life-changing motivational speaker.

My teammates who cracked the lineup didn't do half the work that I did every summer, but they emerged into players who could play in my coach's rotation.

Of all the things that we control as human beings, emergence and the capacity in which it occurs is completely out of our hands.

I was on the team to learn life's processes through the game of basketball. Every, what people describe as profound, word that comes out of my mouth is the result of my not fainting at the designed tribulation that the Creator set in my path. It was the process of unleashing my greatness within me, plain and simple. That's why the Creator says in His Success Manual to "Not faint at my tribulations for you, which is your glory." The sole objective that God has in mind for each and every one of us is that we bring Him glory with our lives. Many people never get this glory that He speaks of in their lives because they simply aren't willing to do what it takes to actualize the dream that was placed in their heart, or they perform an about-face when, in the pursuit of their dream, they begin to encounter real-life obstacles.

Your Creator is a strategist; He knows exactly what you need to go through and overcome in order to become what He already knows you are. He knows that if you become everything He's preordained for you to be, only then will He get the glory from your life that existed before you arrived in this earthly realm. You can't manufacture a plan for your life and say I'm giving God the glory. True paths aren't manufactured, they're discovered! It was no mistake that I wanted to be an NBA player. This is the play that the Creator drew up for my life. He knew that if I wholeheartedly pursued this dream, even in the midst of grim circumstances, that I would become everything He always envisioned my being.

I cannot emphasize enough that the dream in your heart didn't just appear there. It was designed to be pursued for an outcome that only your Creator knows of. He knows from the very onset of your dream that you will have to exercise your faith. Dreams that the Creator put in your heart always have an element of doubt and uncertainty surrounding them. This is where faith comes into play. Your path is manufactured in such a way that you only catch glimpses of your next step. Your view is limited because the Success Manual states, "For without faith it is impossible to please Him." You must have trust in the Creator who framed your world from beginning to end while you're pursuing your dreams. Even if you cannot know how all things will come together, total reliance on your Creator will advance you to your true position in life in spite of what may appear to be impossible odds. Your works, although they are necessary, will not advance you to your next step in your dream pursuit; only faith will!

Any uncommon act of faith is a prelude to an incredible increase. Setting your dreams in motion is an amazing act of faith. If it isn't, then why do so many people live a life of mediocrity when they knowingly have something greater that speaks to them daily? That dream that speaks to them is so far out there that they won't even consider setting it in motion. Ask anyone who's materialized a dream, and they'll tell you it seemed like it was impossible, or at least way out there. What they will also tell you is that the life they now live wouldn't have been possible if they hadn't gone past the doubt in their mind and set their dream in motion.

I discovered something very interesting as I interviewed successful people who recently completed transition stages in their lives. One in particular was a teammate of mine who is now a coach. I asked him questions in such a way that he was totally oblivious of what I was getting at, so I could get straightforward answers. We were talking about our experiences on the hardwood during college, and I asked him if he could now see why he went through the things he went through in his four years of playing basketball in college. He told me, after a brief contemplation, that he wouldn't have discovered his passion to coach if he hadn't gone through the experiences (which weren't always the best) on and off the court during those four years. When he told me that, I then asked him the question I really wanted an answer to: "Would you agree that because you made it through those four years, some things have become naturally instilled in you that are pivotal for your coaching work in this new season of your life?" He responded with a 'yes,' and then went into depth about what he learned during those four years that helped him to function on the level he's at now.

I submit to you today that if you make it through God-ordained tribulation, then some things are naturally instilled in you that are absolutely key to your functioning at your next step in life.

Tribulation is nothing more than life's processes disguised.

As long as you make it through your respective struggles, then you will have the tools to operate on your next level in life. The hard times you encounter are just the Creator's attempt to show you the *real you*. It doesn't matter how you make it through the tribulation-ridden times in life, it just matters that you make it through. I didn't always do everything right during my four years on the court. I wavered plenty of times and got caught up in my logical thinking. But, the bottom line is that I made it through, and I now have the glory talked about in the Success Manual. No, I didn't pass with flying colors, but I didn't faint. The struggle isn't easy by any means, but it's up to you to tap into the God-given strength He's endowed each and every one of you with, to make it through your rough spots and enter into your victory.

————◆————

Tribulation as an Opportunity

Precedents renew the mind. Several precedents must be established in order to achieve greatness. Tribulation (and the ability to overcome that tribulation) is what the Creator sets before you so that your mind may be renewed, and then your identity can be unveiled to you. Yes, overcoming tribulation renews your mind so that the new wine of your destiny can be poured into the renewed skins of your mind. You won't lie dormant in a cellar. Your wine is your gift to this world. Your Creator knows exactly who has a glass awaiting you! Trust that your tribulation is renewing your mind and molding your perception of the world around you in such a way that your new wine won't be tainted by your old way of thinking. The Success Manual clearly states that "you can't put new wine in old skins."

Every experience is making your wine that much sweeter, your gift that much more refined as you emerge victorious from periods of tribulation! Your identity cannot be unveiled to you until the time is right. Press toward your dreams, overcome the universe's obstacles, and you'll collide head-on with your destiny. Trust the Creator and His orchestration of events in your life, and have faith that they are making you who He knows you were before you arrived in this earthly realm. If you make it through your distillation, you are someone's most refined glass of wine. People pay top dollar for fine wine!

Finishing Grace

When you're nearing the end of the struggle phase in the pursuit of your dream, or just at the latter end of any tribulation-ridden time in your life, you have what I call finishing grace. The pressure is on you the most when you're nearing the end of your struggle and on the verge of your victory! This pressure has many facets, mainly mental. This is the point when your struggle is seemingly overwhelming, and you're just hoping it will come to a head. Phrases like, "How much more can I take?" cross your mind. I'm here to tell you that, at this point, you are on the verge of actualizing your dream! Your Creator has designed this tribulation so it will instill in you what he needs in order for you to function in your respective areas of victory. He knows the intensity of the struggle, and in all fairness, He has given you the grace to see it through.

When people are telling you things like, "I just don't understand how you've withstood this thing for so long. How do you do it?" you can tell them that the struggle is an opportunity for your Creator to show Himself to you and those around you. There is an ordained audience that watches you go through the phases of dream pursuit. When you make it through extreme tribulation, yes, God is instilling things in you, but you're also solidifying a legacy by doing what is seemingly impossible to you and those around you. This is why the awareness of finishing grace is so important. You have a supernatural endowment that will come over you as you're nearing the finish line. I don't care how battered and beaten you are from your struggles, there's always victory on the other side. When you're approaching the realm of finishing grace, in all actuality you should have quit by now. You've been through enough, to the point where people wouldn't even be mad at you if you did. You may appear to be destitute in your situation and beyond resuscitation but this is when your Creator shows you and your ordained audience who He really is! Your Creator's only desire for you is that you become everything He already knows you are. So when the pressures of life seem overwhelming, know that He will carry you across the finish line into your victory. If your endowment from above doesn't increase at the latter end of your struggle, then the pressure will take you out. The design is that you really do walk on water and accomplish the impossible so that people will know it wasn't you who did it, but your Father in heaven. A completed journey, from struggle to victory, will ingrain these beliefs in you and the people around you.

This isn't something I've read—well it is, in a sense—this is the script of my life. I played four years of Division I basketball and barely touched the floor. I was a talented player, to say the least, but I rarely played. From my freshmen year to my senior year my teammates and coaches alike would tell me things like, "We just don't understand how you keep a smile on your face despite your condition. We've seen so many players in your predicament, and they just don't respond the way you have. How do you do it? How do you continue to work harder in the midst of such grim circumstances? What drives you?" At times, even I didn't understand what kept me going. Ultimately, I knew God was with me, but I couldn't give anyone an explanation as to how I increased my training regimen every summer in the pursuit of my seemingly hopeless hoop dreams. Especially going into my senior season without having logged any significant minutes. It had to be a kind of grace that was carrying me across the finish line.

Toward the end of my senior year, reality eventually set in and my attitude shifted. I felt I had been wronged my entire career, to have been recruited as a full-scholarship athlete and not touch the floor. And often, when I did get some playing time, I would score as many points as the minutes I played. At the end of my senior year I almost threw in the towel. Something kept me going, though, and that something was the Creator's grace. He knew that there were people watching and that His name was at stake. Your tribulation is a testament to the world of your Father in heaven. I was falling apart at the end of my senior year, but I didn't quit. When the last buzzer went off, signaling the end of my collegiate basketball career, my fellow seniors each let the tears flow. I didn't have any to shed. My ducts were dry.

Days after my senior season ended, my coach was let go as the men's basketball coach of our university. He gave each player a call telling them about his situation. My call came while I was back at home in Maryland on spring break. He briefly told me what had happened and then said words to me I'll never forget, "You persevered, you son-of-a-buck, you persevered. I'll always remember that about you."

When I say you have an ordained audience, this is drawn directly from my life experiences. When you make it through uncommon adversity, you're doing more than you'll ever know. Whatever you may be going through, even though it is seemingly impossible to see it to the end, it is bigger than you. Other people need you to make it through your respective struggles.

Every completed endeavor is a prelude to truth, a truth that your Creator knew about you before this world was spoken into existence, but needs you to realize in order to proceed to your next step in life. Life is a series of truths that represent the truth of who you are. How you make it through the challenges that life sets before you is what people will remember about you when it's all said and done. Don't think it strange when people say things like, "I'll always remember that about you." Truth is undeniable! Every period of tribulation is an opportunity to solidify another piece of your grand legacy. Create substance in your life, so the preacher won't have to stand above you and lie when you make your exit.

The Struggle

At my dream's onset
I did not sign up for this
But your true identity
Emerges in the abyss

That deep dark corner
Things no way you envisioned
Your Creator is sculpting His diamond
To shine with precision

How will you grace your life's stage
With thoughts of your true identity
Internal dialogue still does wage

I once heard that tribulation
Introduces a man to himself
When your storms pass
Before your Creator you will be knelt

As you attest to the victory

That did await

Yes, through your struggle

Your Creator did mold and shape

As you look in the mirror

Adjacent a more glorified state

Which could never have been bestowed

If you performed an about-face

So the next time you think

This cross I cannot bear

Know you're capable and distinct

Eye-to-eye with adversity you can stare

And know the victory was yours

Even before creation

Such is common to man

To never encounter unconquerable temptation

Notes and Insights

Notes and Insights

THE VICTORY

This is when you've made it through your struggle phase. You might be battered and bruised, or passed with flying colors, or you fall somewhere in between; the bottom line is: YOU MADE IT!

In the victory stage, there is an overwhelming feeling of relief, which then turns to excitement until the dream, struggle, and victory cycle repeats itself. Life is nothing more than a series of glorified recurrences. Your Success Manual states that you will go from faith to faith, and glory to glory. You will repeatedly be placed in recurring situations that require you to exercise an increasing amount of faith. There is more at stake with each repetition of the cycle, because there is an increasing level of glory that will come to your life at the end.

Draw from Your Victories!

A new precedent concerning the way you live will have been subconsciously established at the end of each victorious dream pursuit.

During the entire time from when you set your dreams in motion, until the time they actualize themselves, there is doubt resonating in your unconscious mind as to whether you can become everything your heart is telling you that you will be. After the victory is established, your unconscious mind then takes hold of this victory and replaces your old doubtful thinking about whether you could achieve your respective marks with a certainty that you are everything that your heart was telling you that you were all along.

This is where the precedent comes into play. We all make decisions from reference points that dwell in the realm of our unconscious mind. If victory resides where doubt once did, then a new reference point of success also resides in the same place. This new reference point now serves as the precedent your subconscious will grab hold of the next time you encounter a time of severe tribulation in your life. There are several precedents that must be established on your rise to the top. You need reference points because the intensity of situations increases as your life progresses. If you don't have something that is evidential in the realm of your subconscious to refer to when life begins to overwhelm you once again, you're looking at an uphill battle. That's why the Success Manual states, "from faith to faith, and glory to glory." Life is a progression, and precedents are the universe's way of showing you your greatness, so it can bestow upon you your next step to your place within it. This precedent is the new skin of your mind that the Success Manual talks about; your next step in life is the universe's wine that it pours into you. The universe doesn't waste one drop of its wine. This is why its wine isn't poured into your skin unless a certainty is there that the wine and your skin can safely cohabitate.

Successful people get to a point where they've overcome so much and seen the new level of life that awaits them on the other side of the struggle so many times that they actually begin to embrace tribulation as a prelude to the discovery of another level of genius and greatness.

———›‹———

You're Only as Successful as Your Last Victory

Considering the recurring nature of life, it's safe to say that you're only as successful as your last reference point, which is created by your last victory. According to Harvard Business School professor Gerald Zaltman, 95 percent of our decision-making takes place in the subconscious mind. When you find yourself in the tight spots of life in which the world seems to be closing in on you, it's more than beneficial to refer back to the last point in your life where you were in a similar position. This, in turn, gives you a belief that you can overcome whatever obstacle it is you are facing. This belief creates hope in the midst of your adversity, no matter what it looks like. The natural circumstances surrounding your adversity, which may not be favorable to the desired outcome of your dream, were the evidence of your mind's outcome. When a belief is created through drawing back to your last victory, your circumstantial evidence contrary to your dream is eradicated and replaced with a hope and a knowing that your outcome will be similar to or exceed the one that came at the end of your last struggle.

Subconscious reference points are the key to a life of continuous success. Hope and expectancy in the midst of adversity are the evidence that your subconscious will grab hold of, as long as you make it through the struggle and enter into your victory!

———›‹———

Emotion Creates Motion

You must use your past victories to stir up the emotion that propels you through the struggles of life. At every level, there's a new struggle that awaits you. We're in the victory stage, so let's maintain a victorious mindset. At every level there's a new process that awaits you. This process reveals itself in the form of a struggle. Naturally, as human beings, we're driven by emotion. Often times I see people break through seemingly impossible odds by stirring up an emotion that replaces their once-lingering doubt. When you find yourself in a tight spot in life that seems to be overwhelming, take a time-out. Think clearly about the last time you found yourself in a similar situation. Replay every facet of this previous situation; re-live the moment! Feel your struggle! Feel the emotions that consumed you as your situation seemed to be overwhelming you! Feel the pain you seemingly couldn't break through! Yes, feel the emotions you felt as you walked out of your struggle and into your victory! Feel the relief and happiness you felt as you saw the glorious state that awaited you on the other side. Feel the deep knowing you had that your situation didn't compare to the breakthrough that awaited you on the other side.

Channel all of this emotion and apply it to your current, seemingly impossible situation. Let this emotion show you that whatever light affliction you may be facing, it is nothing more than an illusion. But, as you emerge and view this period of affliction in hindsight, the affliction, more often than not, pales in comparison with the victory that always surfaces. See your affliction for what it is—the process of molding you into the glorious person who evolved from your last period of tribulation. Let this new emotion of victory consume you until you are ready to not just go through whatever it is you're facing, but to catapult your way through your struggle and into the victory that you know awaits! When the situations of life seem to be getting the best of you, you always have a victory to fall back on. If you don't, seize every period of tribulation as an opportunity to establish a reference point of victory that will help you accelerate through any situation life presents you. Let your victorious emotions create the momentum that will carry you through the hard times in the pursuit of your dream. You have everything you need inside of you to achieve your dreams—every knowing, every victory, every reference point! It's up to you to make these elements work for you and allow them to propel you in the direction of your victory! You have more than what it takes!

The Victory

Battered and bruised
Or passing with flying colors
A milestone to your mantle
Yes, you've added another

Who knew such a glorious state
Was on the other side of the struggle
Above your adversity you did levitate
Peace in your spirit, where there was unending tussle

Humbled
Apologetic with conviction
Victory reveals all truths
One being the definition of a light affliction

If we know what did await
We would gladly go through
The toughest time of my life
Result: A book contract at twenty-two

Tribulation truly

Is nothing more than life's processes disguised

As you emerge triumphant

A testament to your Creator, confounding the wise

You've earned it

So savor its taste

And always know

After tribulation, your finest hour awaits

Notes and Insights

FEAR, DOUBT, AND OPPOSITION ARE THE UNIVERSE'S ATTEMPT TO SHOW YOU YOUR GREATNESS

COURAGE IS RESISTANCE TO FEAR, MASTERY OF FEAR—
NOT ABSENCE OF FEAR. MARK TWAIN

Fear, doubt, and opposition must be present in order to show you your greatness. These elements must present themselves to you, because if they weren't in place there would be no need to exercise your faith. Faith is the *only* thing that pleases your Creator. Faith in Him that He has enabled you to overcome any adversity is what pleases Him and allows you to be advanced to your next step in life, as well as in your dream pursuit.

The subconscious mind is real. It is the most influential force that drives you, even though you aren't aware of it. The Success Manual talks of "renewing your mind after the image of Him that created him." Let's expose fear, doubt, and opposition in the light in which they should be viewed. These elements will do one of two things (especially when coupled with the intensity of life in general). They will either consume you and force you to turn around in the pursuit of your dreams, or they will force you to confront them head-on and overcome them. When you overcome them, you have the necessary conception of yourself that the Creator wants you to have, so that you will know and understand the true image He has endowed you with before you arrived here in this earthly realm.

That's why I repeatedly emphasize the need to overcome tribulation, because it is the gateway to your discovering things about yourself that you've had all along, and that will exist for eternity. You must gain an awareness of your *real self* in order to operate in your true greatness.

Overcoming fear, doubt, and opposition eliminates the "What ifs" of life and replaces them with "What's next?" It's "What's next?" because when you accomplish the very thing that you and others said you couldn't do, there simply is no "What if." You now have a conception of yourself, in whatever arena you and others doubted you in, that is in perfect harmony with the Creator's conception of you that represents a truth of you. Notice I didn't say "the truth." The truth is the legacy that you leave, which is composed of truths you found out about yourself along life's journey, truths that would remain foreign to you had you not overcome your respective fears, doubts, and opposing forces.

Your Creator allowed you to be the one sperm out of 400 million creative options so you could be the one to achieve greatness. No one arrived here in this earthly realm to just exist and conform to societal norms; that's a ridiculous assumption! Your Creator's only wish for you every day when He wakes you up is that you gain an awareness of the person He's predestined you to be. When you look in the mirror every morning, all you see is you and the conception of yourself that your life experiences have molded your thinking into. God, looking at you through the eyes of His Son, sees a perfect person with brilliance, genius, greatness, and destiny. He's thinking, "If they could just replace their conception of themselves with My knowing of who they are, then they would truly live life at its optimum." He's set up processes on Earth that will instill in you that knowing of who you really are. A major part of these processes are fear, doubt, and opposition. Overcome these, and you will see your very brilliance, genius, and greatness evolving right...before....your eyes!

———•◦•———

Why Do People Doubt Me?

People doubt you for one of two reasons: they either genuinely believe you cannot achieve your dream, or they are intimidated by the knowledge that you exude the necessary characteristics to achieve your dream. Don't feel bad when people doubt you. It's just the way it is! If Jesus Christ, the greatest man to have ever walked the Earth, faced opposition from others—even his parents—concerning who He was, then what makes you think you are exempt? Jesus was plain old Jesus, the son of Mary and Joseph, until word got back to His hometown of the miracles that preceded Him. You, too, will have to operate at a level of absolute genius for those closest to you to be able to eradicate the conceptions of the person they saw you as while you were growing up.

Your gift and dream is your genius, and it is the best possible thing you can give to the universe. It represents the truth of who you are. It is given to you to operate in and solve some sort of problem on Earth. Considering that your genius is an extension of God—the only perfect existence—it will have a profound impact on the world around you. This impact will precede you and be a testament to everyone, including those closest to you. In essence, it will make them see you as not being the same, and as existing in an undeniable truth. If your greatness precedes you and people still won't acknowledge the true you, then there is nothing you can do. Operating within your gift and within your dream is you fulfilling a call that existed for eternity; it is undeniable truth! If the people who know you are not convinced, they're just cynics and doubters!

There is another breed of person who can see your infinite possibilities more vividly than you can. Whenever you operate from within a gift, it has impact. Some people operate in gifts unknowingly, and they have an impact on the people around them. You unknowingly operate in these gifts because they are effortless and natural. Other people can see your effortless gifts and the potential greatness that accompanies them. People will knowingly express doubt to you concerning your abilities as a result of their own insecurity within themselves. Even some friends who should encourage you in your endeavors will attempt to prevent you from achieving the greatness they know is right around the corner, if only you could see yourself from an out-of-the-frame perspective. Some people are so intimidated by your potential that they will make it their job to kill your dream by speaking venomous words to you about it. People don't want you to surpass them. I hate to be the one to break it to you, but this is what you will encounter on your way to the top.

Two of my best friends were basketball players in college. In discussions about the game and people we've played with, the subject came up, in separate conversations with both of them, about players with potential. One of my friends spoke of a teammate he played with in high school. Keep in mind that this player played the same position as my friend did, and so this player was detrimental to my friend getting the playing time he wanted. My friend said, "He had all the tools to become great. He was six feet ten inches with an uncanny shooting touch for his size. He was strong and athletic too! I could never tell him this because I knew we played the same position, even though I knew he wasn't playing up to his potential. Thinking back, my words would have probably helped him because he was close to me and respected me."

My second friend and I had the same conversation. He spoke about a teammate he played with in college. The scenario is identical to the one just mentioned. He said, "This guy was taller and more athletic than me. He was soft, though. I knew that if he *put his mind to it* he could have been really good. He wasn't playing up to his potential, but I couldn't tell him; we played the same position."

How many people around you have been speaking negative words to you about your dreams? How many people can you now see are just intimidated by your greatness? Don't look at the person, check the motive. I'll guarantee that in some capacity, you both play similar positions in life. These positions could be financial, family-related, occupational—anything.

Don't be that person who holds back on sharing information with other people concerning their potential and ability. What you make happen for others will happen for you. In all actuality, no one is detrimental to your achieving what it is the Creator placed you here to do. The Success Manual says that "We are ambassadors of Christ." An ambassador is a high-ranking political representative of another country sent to reside in a territory as a representative of their native land.

We, as human beings, are ambassadors sent into this earthly realm as a representative of our Father's Kingdom. We've each been assigned a territory to occupy what is reflected in our dreams. No one can infiltrate your space, and you can't enter anyone else's. No one should be a threat to you! You can't do what they do...and they can't do what you do! Point blank! Help people actualize their dreams. Uplift them; help them get over life's humps. If you make this happen for others, then the universe will make the same allowances for you! Life is truly a 360-degree circle!

Fear, Doubt, and Opposition

Fear, doubt, and opposition
Your enemy's trinity
But overcoming this three-headed monster
Introduces you to divinity

No one is exempt
They dwell in our being
But through faith
Eyes fixated on vision
That's what we're seeing

Why do they doubt me?
This is my dream
They know you can do it
And mediocrity is their team

They want you in their boat
Sinking with every passing year
Unfulfilled in life
Crying internal tears

Fear, doubt and opposition
Let me out of your grips
To the majority
I no longer want to be joined at the hip

Set your dream in motion
And its grips will tighten
Oh, but as separation occurs
You will truly be enlightened

I had no idea
I was capable of this
Because your true identity
Is beyond its grips

Move beyond this trio
Which keeps so many grounded
Your limitless possibilities
Yes, you'll undoubtedly be astounded

Notes and Insights

The Universe Is Inviting You In: Your Best Life Possible Awaits You

THE COMPANY YOU KEEP

YOUR INNER CIRCLE CREATES YOUR OUTER ATMOSPHERE.   MATTHEW C. HORNE

I've heard every motivational speaker say, "You are a sum total of the five people you spend the most time with." This is absolutely true. These similarities range from personality to income. MIT did a study that concluded that you will make to within three to four thousand dollars of what your five closest friends make. Relax. Don't start kicking people out of your house!

If you want to see your future, look no further than your friends. Every facet of their lives most likely will be duplicated in yours. I look at relationships from the standpoint of the "social milieu." A social milieu is a social setting that is stabilized by governing norms that all of its inhabitants must abide by. In order to function within the milieu, you must conform to the norms of the group, or else you jeopardize your position within it. You must look, act, and smell like everyone in the group, or else you will be phased out.

If you have a vision that you're pressing toward that requires you to not be able to conform to the norms of the group, then a problem occurs. Do you continue on with your vision and leave the group, or do you stay, and conform to the norms and experience the discontentment associated with an unfulfilled vision?

If you truly are pressing toward a vision, then naturally, seasons change in your life. In order to maximize the changing seasons in life, you have to surround yourself with like-minded people who are pressing toward greatness as well. There is always someone you can keep company with, every stop along the way to your destiny.

The beauty of it is that someone does not have to be at arm's length in order for you to keep company with them. I encourage my clients to surround themselves with people who are at levels that they envision themselves rising to. This is easily done through books and audio presentations. Sit at their feet and have conversations. Take the knowledge they relay and apply it to your life. It's no coincidence the Success Manual says "iron sharpens iron." Surround yourself with people who help you go forward in life. You're either going forward or backward at all times in life. Stagnation is an illusion. If you aren't progressing, then you're undoubtedly regressing.

If you want to live life in a progressive state, then choose your friends according to their ability to help you maintain a mindset that is conducive to your achieving your vision. Successful people recognize the changing seasons in their lives and make the necessary adaptations to function at the level of their new season.

The actualization of your vision must be the parameters used when selecting the company you keep. Do these people aid you in achieving your vision, or do they hinder it? Letting go of friends who are detrimental to your success is hard for the majority of society, because the majority of society doesn't have a vision. The key to continually surrounding yourself with people who are beneficial to you is to have a vision that has consumed you to the point that anything detrimental to it must be cut off. Vision is the key to life.

———➤•◄———

Streeeeeetch Yourself

I have a friend who is preparing for the upcoming basketball season. He plays at the Division III level, and he asked me what he could do to improve as a player over the summer. I recollected my experiences as a collegiate basketball player and told him to find people who are better than he is, and seek them out. We are privileged enough to live fewer than thirty minutes away from the University of Maryland, so that gives him access to the level of basketball player that he needs to surround himself with.

He did exactly what I told him regarding playing with superior talent, and was quite surprised with his ability to compete with athletes at such a high level.

Success is nothing more than gaining an awareness of what's already inside of you!

In order for this awareness to take place, you must be in the vicinity of greatness. My friend hasn't been the same player since that day. His confidence has soared, and his work ethic has intensified. He now understands what it takes to play at the elite levels in basketball. He not only played pick-up basketball, but he stuck around and got to see what other habits these players had. He always had the potential to be that good, he just wasn't aware of it.

You are born successful, and you die successful. Right now, as you're reading the words on these pages, you're as successful as you're ever going to be. Will you put yourself in the vicinity of the people you need to in order to gain an awareness of the potential that's already inside of you? The choice is yours!

Greatness doesn't approach you, you approach it! Those players from the University of Maryland didn't need anything my friend had to offer. They had everything he needed in order to go to the next level in his player development. He went to their open gym and sought them out. You must be in the energy orbit of people who operate at the level that you envision for yourself in order to find the clues of their success. Success always leaves clues!

There must be an element of reality when choosing your surrounding company. You must first take inventory within yourself to see where you really are, and where you know in your heart you should be. This will show you clearly the type of people you should seek out. Humbling yourself and acknowledging the people who will benefit you gets the ball rolling in the direction of your best possible life.

⎯⎯➤◆◄⎯⎯

The Power of Association

I recently attended the FraserNet PowerNetworking Conference, where a prominent theme was that of the power of associations that are beneficial to you in going to new levels in your professional and personal development. I can still hear the motivational legend George Fraser saying, "I hang with people who have big cheese, even more than me." He understands the importance of key associations that will make you play up to their level of excellence.

Mediocrity creates a glass ceiling. There is an unspoken alliance that keeps you at a level where you don't surpass the norms of your milieu and jeopardize your position within it. The glass ceiling is real! It's no coincidence that television shows such as *Friends* became such a hit in the 1990s and beyond. Everyone can relate to the idea of a social milieu and the norms that are associated with it.

Tony Robbins, a world-renowned authority in self-development, said that he was stretched by a group of men who flew jets and took exotic trips at the drop of a hat. They schooled him on how to go to new levels in every facet of life. He humbled himself and conformed to the norms of the group and sat at the feet of the people within the group. He had not yet reached their level of excellence, but one act of humility enabled him to go to that next level in his development as a person.

In any group you must conform to the norms in order to solidify your position within it. Find a group with norms that are beneficial to your functioning at the level you envision for yourself. More importantly, choose your associations according to the seasons in your life. If you're starting a business and all of your friends have 9-to-5 jobs, then their behaviors will naturally clash with yours, especially if you want to make that business successful. Getting off work and having a few drinks is the norm when working 9 to 5. When building a business, eighteen-hour days are nothing out of the ordinary. It's easy to see where the philosophies clash.

Every milieu has a philosophy. You're only as successful as the philosophy you adopt. A person's philosophy exemplifies who they are and validates their standing in life. Every action you make and every thought you have originates from your personal philosophy. That's why MIT proved that you make within three to four thousand dollars of your closest friends. Philosophies produce results. Just find the group that has the results and a philosophy that is conducive to your achieving the results you want out of life, and there lies the recipe for success.

The Success Posture

I had a teammate in college who was 6 feet 11 inches tall. He was my best friend on the team, and naturally we hung out together. I'm only 6 feet 5 inches, but when I was with him I was every inch of that 6 feet 5. There was a subconscious pull from his stature that made me determined to measure up, in a sense, whenever I was around him. Needless to say, my posture was at its best when I was around him. We are ever-evolving beings—we'll never completely arrive until our last breath is taken. At every season in life, your posture must be at its best in order to maximize that season. Associations with people, like me with my 6-feet-11-inches teammate, will ensure that your posture remains at its best at all times.

I made another interesting observation concerning posture during my time in college. I noticed that my posture wasn't the same when I hung around with people who weren't taller than me. I wasn't as upright in my posture as I could be because no one was stretching me to their height. My shoulders were a bit more round and my back wasn't as straight. It's as if I was subconsciously apologizing for my God-given height so that I could accommodate people who weren't as tall as I was. If you surround yourself with people who don't share your same gargantuan vision, then you will undoubtedly find yourself apologizing for dreaming beyond their status in life. Do you really think the people in the MIT study don't have visions that surpass their surrounding friends? Of course not! It's just the unspoken alliance that requires you to not excel, or else you jeopardize your standing within the group and face possible resentment for breaking the glass ceiling. I've seen people not drive their new cars in order to make people feel better. I've seen people move into brand-new houses and not tell a soul. In essence, they were apologizing for their success. There is only one circumstance that warrants an apology when it comes to your dreams—when you never fulfill your God-given dream that your Creator has endowed you with. When you hold onto that dream and never position yourself to actualize what your Creator chose for you to do, then an apology is definitely in order.

You're postured for success when you feel left out and you don't have the amenities of the people who surround you. If you are constantly being stretched, then your subconscious mind is unceasingly thinking of ways to exploit your inner genius and brilliance so you can be afforded the amenities of your surrounding company. The company you keep should have an enticing menu of success, or else you'll resign yourself to the dollar menu!

———>•<———

The Placebo Effect

You must fight negative self-talk and doubt at every level in life. It takes multiple positive comments to eradicate just one negative comment. When you share an idea of what you can do with someone who doesn't share your same vision in life, then they automatically won't be able to relate to you. They'll shoot your dreams down in an instant and won't think twice about it. A person's opinion of you is a derivative of their own philosophy. If you accept the opinion of someone, you adopt their philosophy, and thus duplicate the results in their life. People simply think you can't do things in life because they have yet to do them. If their opinion becomes your reality, then yes, you will duplicate exactly what they've done in the arena of your dream—NOTHING!!!

A funny thing happened when I told someone I respected and admired that I was writing a book. They said, "What makes you think you can write a book? I haven't even written one yet." I was flowing and the book was writing itself until that point. My writing came to a screeching halt for nearly two months after hearing that comment. But, as you can see, I got a reality check and finished the book. And you know what? That person still hasn't written their book. Do you get the picture now? If you allow a person's opinion of you to become a reality, then you accept the reality of that person.

The right company reshapes your thinking into something that is more conducive to your achieving success in life. Ideas involving dreams are always "way out there" according to societal standards. If you simply position yourself with strategic associations, then the story in your mind is constantly formulated in such a way that your dream is possible! Every season means new associations, because every season has an increasing level of productivity. Dreamers who keep company with dreamers enable each other to deliver the dream that resides inside them.

There is a process from conception to delivery. Every level is a new time of conception. The right associations give your dream the care it needs in order to deliver your gift to this world. The story in your mind concerning the possibilities of your dream will determine whether your dream will ever arrive in this earthly realm.

Right now, as you're reading the words on these pages, you have all the potential to be as successful as you will ever be. Success that is extracted from your inner being and made manifest in this earthly realm is what society defines as success. If the people in your life don't enable you to maintain an awareness of the dream you're carry-ing inside of you, then naturally your behavior will create conditions that are unfavorable to your delivering that dream. But, if the aware-ness is in place, then the prevailing thought concerning every deci-sion you make will be based on whether it is beneficial or harmful to your dream.

Dreamers are few and far between, and the higher you go in life, the harder it gets to find people who actually want to continue ascend-ing. This is why the average millionaire spends thousands of dollars a year on self-improvement. Millionaires keep company with books and audio presentations that keep the story in their mind formulated in such a way that their dreams are never forgotten. They go to seminars with empowering messages geared toward their limitless possibilities. I was at a Tony Robbins conference recently, and he asked the question "Who in here is a business owner?" Over 75 percent of the crowd raised their hand. Find the company you want to keep, or the company you settle for will dead-bolt the lock on the door to your best life possible!

The Company You Keep

They are a reflection
Of you
A sum total of the five closest
Does this theory hold true

Every group
With their governing philosophy
Has a direct correlation
To your potential's velocity

Do you want to soar
To unseen heights
Or are you comfortable
Settled and parked in life

Keep company with people
At your vision's plateau
They're accessible
Even through books you get to know

The bottom line
You must be postured for success
The desired result in their life
You must be able to attest

Never settle
Sink or swim is the motto
Your company
Should keep your brain on full throttle

When I listen to speakers
They introduce me to me
As I have blessed assurance
No theory, a motivator I was born to be

You must ask yourself
Where in life do you want to go?
The journey begins
With finding people
Doing it at the plateau

Notes and Insights

PERPETRATE TO PERPETUATE

Some time ago, I was watching a Kobe Bryant DVD and several things jumped off the screen and caught my attention. The Michael Jordan comparisons were startling and permeated the entire DVD. It is obvious to me that Kobe Bryant studied Michael Jordan's on- and off-the-court characteristics as if he'd majored in it in college. The tendencies the two players share is evident to an unmistakable degree.

Everyone wants to know, "What am I here for; what is my purpose; how do I find my true identity?" The answer is simple. Follow the dream in your heart, and try to duplicate the actions of someone who is at the top of where you envision yourself going. Kobe Bryant could have imitated any player in the NBA, but he chose the best one to have ever graced a basketball court. He adopted his work ethic, and in essence, adopted the philosophy of Michael Jordan. There's no need to reinvent the wheel. The universe is aligned in such a way that whatever kind of model you need, in terms of successful precedents, is laid out before you. It's up to you to seek it out!

The average man has difficulty asking for directions when he's lost
on the road, and the same holds true when a man is lost in life.

You need direction at the onset of any dream pursuit, or else you're facing an uphill battle! The direction you need is simply found in mirroring the tactics of the person who epitomizes the desired end you have for your life. Success rarely can be found in innovation—it is in duplication that success lies. If your way of doing things has gotten you the results that you and your heart know you should have, more power to you. If not, your desired results are no further away than the perpetrating, emulating, and implementing of the successful tactics of a success model until you can perpetuate what you and your heart know you should have.

When Kobe Bryant first entered the NBA, he was ridiculed for his uncanny imitation of Michael Jordan. He was called names like "Heir Jordan" and "Carbon-Copy Mike." I too thought I was watching a younger version of Michael Jordan. He was "perpetrating" to say the least. But something strange began to happen as the years progressed in the career of Kobe Bryant. He began to perpetuate the accomplishments of the man he once emulated. The championship rings, the MVPs, the dunk contest championship, and the list goes on.

The mitigating factor that keeps people from attaining success through duplication is pride, and the deeply imbedded fear that they will somehow lose themselves in the process. Think it no strange thing that the Bible says "pride goeth before destruction." Destruction manifests itself when you don't become everything your Creator has intended you to be. It's an uncommon act of humility to realize that your way of doing things just won't cut it, and that there's someone out there who's already paved the way. Any uncommon act of humility is a prelude to incredible increase. You will have to lose yourself in the process, but you'll emerge with a clearer sense of who you *truly* are. To die is to gain.

When I see Kobe Bryant now, I don't see "Carbon-Copy Mike," I see the player we've come to know as Kobe Bryant. I see a player who looks less and less like Mike; I see a player who's truly found his identity as a player. The on-the-court mannerisms are seldom mentioned anymore. The only comparisons I seem to hear these days about the two players are from the standpoint of performance and accolades. It is believed that Kobe is poised to surpass Mike in many ways. None of this could have been set in motion had Kobe not humbled himself and done due diligence on the greatest player in the arena he was in.

Each of you has a dream, and a complementing genius that will enable that dream to thrive. Cultivated genius is what makes it to the bright lights.

Kobe and Michael are two of the most gifted athletes on the planet, but it is often overlooked that they are also two of the hardest working. It's no coincidence that, for either one of them, anything less than the taste of champagne at the end of the season is a disappointment.

Your Creator is constantly putting things and events in your path that will enable you to gain an awareness of what's already inside of you. When you truly gain an awareness of your true self and operate in it, you give your Creator the glory He intended to get from your life when He chose you to be born. The sole objective for our Creation is that we give our Creator glory. There is nothing you can do to manufacture this glory—it can only be discovered! Perpetrating to perpetuating is one of the many tools your Creator has laid in your path to help you gain an awareness of who you truly are. Walking in your God-given destiny is the closest you'll ever come to perfection.

Every new idea, dream, and endeavor is an attempt from your Creator to reveal another part of your true identity to you. He is constantly giving you ideas and strategically placing you in situations that introduce you to your true self, if seen through to completion. There's always a new level to be reached as long as you have breath in your body. Embarking on new dreams that the Creator places inside of you is what enables you to constantly discover new facets of your true self. Every new level of truth you walk in is a greater testament to your Creator in Heaven. Your life is crafted with a design for you to be a testament to your Creator. Each manifested level of truth is another episode in the screenplay of your life—all you have to do is follow whatever dream is in your heart at any given time, and you automatically get the starring role. Your Creator, who acts as director, handpicked you for the role, and knows it is yours for the taking if you just show up—no audition needed!

Awareness is the result of strategic positioning. When you find someone doing what you envision yourself doing and you adopt their philosophy, you position yourself to gain an awareness of your true self. Your Creator's only desire for you is for you to walk in His truth concerning your life. Truth comes about when you are, as Dr. Wayne Dyer would say, "in spirit." Many of the ideas and concepts that have led to the success of the people you study will be eerily similar to the thoughts and ideas you have. This lets you know you're on the right track, and makes your negative self-talk sign the permission slip releasing you to explore new facets of your greatness.

Every decision you make originates in the realm of your subconscious mind. Your subconscious mind doesn't set plans in action until it has tangible evidence that the plans are possible. Seeing firsthand how someone has done it from start to finish is all the evidence your subconscious mind needs to get the ball rolling in the direction of your best life possible.

If You Don't Know, Just Ask!

When you seek out people who are doing what you envision your-self doing, you're doing nothing more than asking how they've attained the results in their life. Even if they aren't accessible enough to ask them personally, pick up their book and ask them questions. They'll un-doubtedly answer you! They'll give you advice based on their philoso-phy that has worked for them. Implement their answers into your way of doing things, and you will afford yourself the privilege of ordering from the menu of their success. Remember, you're only as successful as the philosophy you adopt.

Studying people who set the bar for excellence in your field will put you on the accelerated track to your destiny. Just as Christ has paid the price for our sins, you have predecessors who have paid the price for your success. You will inevitably get some bumps and bruises along the way to your dreams, but many of them can simply be avoided by observing those precedents that the universe has set before you.

I've come to learn that great people get to a point where they've at-tained so much in life that they just want to duplicate themselves. This is when they offer training, write books, and explore different avenues of duplication. The next generation comes behind them and adopts the same concepts with a personal twist and continues the cycle of uncommon success to duplication of one's self.

Perpetrate to Perpetuate

It's an uncommon act of humility
To do it another way
If we only knew
This is the accelerated track to finding our way

I see this in Kobe Bryant's imitation
Michael Jordan
The same stage he envisioned himself gracing

So he took a step back
How did he do it?
The greatest of all time
With movements so fluid

Let me study him out
On and off the court mannerism
Everything he encompasses
Lay his destiny's provision

Kobe Bryant

"Carbon Copy Mike" he was called by many

But an accelerated trip to the top

Moved ridicule to envy

No more *Heir* Jordan

His mantle of accomplishments now assimilate

Eerily familiar

To the man he once did imitate

Yes, through duplication

He found his identity

Now on pace to surpass Mike

And rewrite history

It's as simple as

Finding someone who's done it

Doing it your way

Will leave your potential stunted

Notes and Insights

YOU HAVE THE TOOLS TO ACTUALIZE YOUR DREAMS

THEN SAY NOT MAN'S IMPERFECT, HEAV'N IN FAULT;

SAY RATHER, MAN'S AS PERFECT AS HE OUGHT;

HIS KNOWLEDGE MEASUR'D TO HIS STATE AND PLACE,

HIS TIME A MOMENT, AND A POINT HIS SPACE.

IF TO BE PERFECT IN A CERTAIN SPHERE,

WHAT MATTER, SOON OR LATE, OR HERE OR THERE?

THE BLEST TODAY IS AS COMPLETELY SO,

AS WHO BEGAN A THOUSAND YEARS AGO.   ALEXANDER POPE, "AN ESSAY ON MAN,"

Fear is the number-one killer of dreams, point blank! Deep-seated feelings of inadequacy are what keep 95 percent of society in a box.

If you managed to be created by one out of 400 million sperm, don't you think you were created to do more than just conform to the monotonous routine of life? If God chose you, and made over 399 million of your brothers and sisters take a back seat to you, then that's evidence enough that you not only have a dream, but are hard-wired to fulfill it!

"Say Not Man's Imperfect, Heav'n in Fault"

If anyone, including you, relays thoughts of inadequacy to you concerning your dream, then in fact they are saying that your Creator is at fault. They're saying that He separated you from the rest of the pack, placed you in this earthly realm, and didn't equip you to carry out His plan for your life. Be careful what you say about dreams, for they are totally separate from the people who house them. Believe me, you never know who you're sitting next to. People are just vehicles that your Creator uses to manifest His plan on Earth as it is in heaven. Your dream is a perfect extension of Him in you, with instructions to thrive, no matter the circumstance.

"Say Rather, Man's as Perfect as He Ought"

We all have our shortcomings; no one is without legitimate illusions as to why they can't carry out their dreams, but you are perfect as you ought to be.

Whatever your dream is, you have the capability and the capacity to carry it out.

Any internal or external obstacles that appear in the path of your dream have already been overcome for you by your Creator. Life is not fair, but it's fair in the sense that you have everything inside of you to become everything your Creator has predestined you to be.

"His Knowledge Measur'd to His State and Place"

You aren't intelligent enough to carry out the big picture for your life! For you to even get in the theater where the movie of your life is playing, you must operate in a realm of genius. Your Creator doesn't think small by any means. For you to rely on your intelligence alone is to create a ceiling by which you will eventually taper off if you don't discover your genius.

Any ceiling that you manufacture for your life is an enemy to your limitless possibilities.

The vivid depictions of your dream can get so overwhelming at times that you think, "There's no way can I do that." This is a great place to be! This forces you to exit the realm of self-reliance and enter the realm of faith. Your Creator says in His Success Manual, "Without faith, it is impossible to please Him." Your dream is supposed to seem as way out there, because it is. It is way out there beyond your intellect and housed in the realm of genius.

Every dream has an accompanying genius. Your genius is the endowment that your Creator gives you to access His brain so that He can think for you. It can only be accessed through humility and faith—humility in the sense that you know you can't rely solely on yourself to actualize your dreams, and faith in the sense that your Creator has endowed you with the tools to actualize your dreams.

Your measure of knowledge is precisely measured to your space of existence in this universe—your God-given assignment and calling. This is a measure of God's infinite knowledge, given to you so that you'll adequately carry out His plan with no interference from any shortcomings that you might possess. Considering that this knowledge is from the only infallible existence there is, it will far surpass even your highest thought, and translate into genius in this natural realm. There are geniuses in many arenas who've never graduated from college, or even high school, but they somehow confound us when their genius takes effect. It's because they've tapped into knowledge far beyond their greatest areas of intelligence. They've bypassed their natural limitations concerning their life's calling by connecting to supernatural wisdom that was only accessed through faith in a Creator who respected their faith in Him, and who extended His mind to them—which translates to what we've labeled as genius.

The key to success is keeping an in-the-frame perspective. The minute you need to know how it will all come together is the minute you've eradicated your Creator's role as the director in the movie of your life. When you're the director, get ready to bump your head on the ceiling you've set for your life! Relying solely on your intelligence will always create a ceiling on your life. It will keep your mind fixated in this natural realm governed by mediocrity and security, and will without question dead-bolt the lock on the door to your best life possible!

<hr>

"His Time a Moment"

I can hear George Fraser saying it now, "Stay the Course." If you press toward your dreams and don't quit in the middle of the process, then your finest hour awaits you. That is the moment when you can clearly see why all of the obstacles appeared, why things didn't happen according to your schedule; that moment is waiting for you to collide head-on with it. Your time is truly a moment. You can believe by faith up until that point, but when that which others, and even yourself, with negative self-talk, said would never take place actually does happen, you'll have found your space within this universe. These results are what your subconscious mind grabs hold of concerning who you really are. There's no turning back from this point. The precedent has been established for a continual emergence into the person you are destined to be.

You will not just experience success, but you will have commenced your journey to living a life of optimum success. This is when you become, not only who you want to be, nor merely envision yourself being, but rather everything your Creator has predestined you to be. You've entered into your Creator's perfection, and He will take over from this point on; you've entered His graces.

This reference point of success is so important because it allows you to bypass the doubting forces that have plagued you in the past. When you grab hold of who you truly are without harboring any doubts, then facets of yourself that you never knew existed can be unveiled to you. We've talked about the skin of your mind and the universe's wine, but this is when the universe can pour its precious wine of your true identity into the skin that is your mind. This happens because significant reference points of success fortify the skin of your mind in such a way that the wine won't explode it. The universe doesn't waste a drop of its wine. Life is a steady progression. Every instance of success is formulating your mind to receive the next facet of your true identity.

Oh, but your time is but a moment! When you have a dream that you truly believe in, you prepare. This preparation must take place blindly, as circumstances don't indicate whether your dream will ever come to pass. Everyone is on a collision-course with their destiny. You will arrive at a place where your dreams can become a reality. It will truly be a moment. The significance of this moment depends on how prepared you are for it. Listen to that something telling you to prepare for you heart's desires. That something knows that your preparation isn't in vain, but that it is necessary to capture that very moment when your destiny stares you right in the face. Moments are either captured, or they pass you by. The moment will come when you have that chance encounter that will propel you to your dream. That opportunity you've always waited for is just a moment away. Just prepare, prepare, prepare, because your time is truly a moment!

I heard a speaker say, "Being in the right place at the right time and not taking action makes it as if you were never there." I also heard Ona Brown say, "The highest form of faith is preparation." If you truly have faith in your dream, then preparation will accompany it. The Success Manual states that "faith without works is dead," meaning that if you say that you believe in something and do not have the works to validate that belief, the faith that you allegedly possess is nonexistent.

Everyone will find themselves at the right place at the right time. The chance encounter that your soul has longed for since before creation will stare you right in the face, but it's your preparation up to that point that serves as the mitigating factor as to whether you can capture that moment, or have it pass you by.

Whenever there's a dream or desire in your heart, you **must** *prepare. You never know which moment will be your defining moment.*

These are the moments, that when captured, will forever change the definition of who you are. When Michael Jordan hit the game-winning shot in 1984 that solidified the national championship for his University of North Carolina Tar Heels, he was never viewed in the same light again. He emerged from obscurity to absolute prominence in an instant. He undoubtedly captured a moment that changed the definition of who he was forever. Up until that point, he was a country boy from North Carolina who many in his hometown never believed would excel under Hall of Fame coach Dean Smith. But, in an instant, the definition of this country boy was changed forever.

From the outside looking in, all we can see is the moment. Believe me, coming from a background of Division I basketball, I know the amount of preparation that went into that moment. I can clearly see him waking up at 5 a.m. to work out with his coaches. I can see the thousands of jump shots his coaches made him take from the same spot on the floor where he hit the game-winning shot. There was an immense amount of preparation that went into that moment. Your willingness to prepare is what will enable you to capture your defining moment when the bright lights are on you. Michael Jordan, without question, possesses a genius for the game of basketball, but his willingness to cultivate it through preparation is what made him the best.

We all have a genius; cultivated genius is what makes it to the bright lights.

———◦———

"A Point His Space"

The dream that is in your heart is either your IT in life, or it's meant to put you in the vicinity of your TRUE IT—your space within this universe. It's important to embark upon every new endeavor with a focus and an energy that will enable you to see it through to completion.

My die-hard allegiance to my NBA hoop dreams is what led me to motivational speaking. That day in my speech class when I gave a speech paralleling success in the game of basketball to success in life was the moment when I knew that the definition of who I thought I was had changed forever. When my classmates told me that I should be a motivational speaker, their words were pointing me in the direction of my space. I wanted to be an NBA player; but my space, which represented the person I was designed to be, existed in the realm of motivational speaking. This is why Alexander Pope says, "His time a moment, and a point his space." There is a moment that awaits you that will point you in the direction of your space—if it is met with adequate preparation.

———✦———

"If to Be Perfect in a Certain Sphere"

Everyone wants to know—"What is my IT in life?" Your IT is your space in the universe that represents your *certain sphere* of perfection. It is the sphere in this universe in which you will be perfect. Your sphere of perfection never disappears. Your space within this universe is *yours* and no one can ever infiltrate it. You can never measure your ability to achieve your dreams by any natural ability that you have. When it comes to your dream and your space within this universe, you have insight that surpasses any knowledge you will ever accumulate, or currently possess. Most geniuses aren't phenomenal thinkers in every aspect of life. We may perceive them to be, simply because they wow us with their knowledge and ability in a certain sphere. Geniuses battle the same feelings of inadequacy as any common man, because they are common men who've discovered their sphere of perfection.

Michael Jordan exerted the same energy into becoming a baseball player as he did in becoming a great basketball player. He was mediocre at best when playing minor-league baseball, but as close to perfection as we've ever seen in the game of basketball. He tried with all of his might to excel on the baseball diamond, but found that his diamond would only glisten on the basketball court. In the words of

Michael Jordan, "All I am is a basketball player. That's who I am and what I am, and that's all I am."

Your insight concerning a thing is measured to your purpose. I had someone tell me, "For a twenty-three-year-old, you sure do have a lot of insight on life." In that instant, I comprehended what insight really is. Insight, in the traditional sense, is gained through experience or studying; but true insight can be accessed when you're operating in your sphere of perfection, no matter what your age. God has equipped you with the tools needed to excel in the arena of your dream—one of these tools being the ability to come out of yourself and see things from the perfect extension of Himself that He's placed in you. Your knowledge and insight are measured to your state and place. Believe in your dream and the ability to excel in your respective arenas, and you'll find that you can do more than you've ever imagined.

Office . . . Space

In writing a book at the age of twenty-three, I've encountered many people who say that I'm just too young. The *office* of a motivational speaker should be occupied by someone with more experience. "You just haven't lived enough life yet," is an example of the phrases I often hear from people who relay ego-based thoughts of inadequacy toward my dreams and life's calling. It's the ego, that part of us that edges God out, which keeps us confined to our office and never enables us to discover our space within this universe. Yes, realistically speaking, a twenty-three-year-old shouldn't be able to say the things that I do; shouldn't be able to understand life's processes in such a developed manner, but I've left the ego-dominated place of myself that plagues the majority of society, keeping them locked in its box of mundane routine, and tapped into my supernatural source that doesn't regard my age, or many of the other inadequacies I possess. I've tapped into the perfect extension of the only infallible existence there is, and believe that He hasn't confined me to any natural stipulations that qualify me to walk in the office of a motivational speaker. Rather, I embrace my true essence and space within a universe that does not respect this world's governing qualifications of any office. Only my Creator's instructions for me to thrive and become everything He knew I was before creation.

If I were to accept others' ego-based opinions concerning my readiness and ability to become a motivational speaker and author, I would go no further than their opinion concerning my capabilities. This natural world is governed by ego. Ego keeps you perfectly aligned with the world's governing way of mediocrity. That's why I repeatedly emphasize that the Success Manual clearly says that we are "in this world, but not of this world."

We were created by a supernatural God, who in no way respects the governing laws of society. Since He dwells in the realm of the supernatural, our destiny is beyond the capabilities that we possess in the natural realm and is housed accordingly in the supernatural realm. Faith is what enables you to step out of the world around you and truly find your space within the universe. Faith is the permeating theme of my life, as well as this book. So too must it be yours, if you are ever to become what your Creator has intended you to be. Always having faith in your Creator's unlimited supply of supernatural provision, which is *distinctly* measured to your destiny, will *always* keep you in a harmonious state with your Creator. When you've entered the supernatural and done away with any ego-based perceptions that disqualify you from occupying your office, you'll soar above the negative opinions of yourself and others regarding your life's calling, and truly find your space.

The key to staying in the supernatural, where your destiny is housed, is to simply wake up every morning and see yourself from your Creator's perspective—as a supernatural being capable of bringing the super to any natural situation if total reliance is fixed in Him!

If you truly want to soar to higher heights in life, you must keep your mind focused on your space within God's infinite universe. Dwelling on the office of your life's calling will undoubtedly keep you grounded in life, because you'll never totally meet every prerequisite concerning your heart's desires, and even if you do, there's the internal dialogue that casts a shadow of doubt concerning your ability. Whatever it is that you believe in your heart, know that there is a supernatural provision that you can access by keeping your Creator's endless supply of wisdom, insight, and ability at the forefront of your mind. Ego needs natural evidence as to how everything will come together; faith in your Creator is the evidence that enables Him to add His super to your natural and continuously keep you in His supernatural plan on your life. You can have faith in the office, or the space—the choice is yours! Why confine yourself to a cubicle, when every breath you take is the universe's personal invitation to your best life possible?

"What Matter, Soon or Late"

"I'm too old", "I'm too young." If you only knew that you are too perfect! Every morning, when your Creator wakes you up, He sees you as having the ability to carry out the very thing He's put you on this planet to do! He sees that gift inside of you that only you can deliver to this world. If it was too late, then why would He wake you up every morning?

As long as you have breath in your body, you haven't missed it.
Your Creator's most thriving business in this earthly realm is that of
restoration.

He's constantly hoping that you will see yourself as He sees you so that you can gain an awareness of what it is He's placed you here to do. Regardless of your past, regardless of your shortcomings, he simply wants you to prosper. He says it in His Success Manual, "I wish above all things that thou mayest prosper and be in health, even as thy soul prospereth."

You were spirit and soul before you arrived here in this earthly realm. They know things about you that you don't know about yourself. That unrest you feel within originates in the realm of your soul area if you aren't doing what you were placed here to do. The only way to experience soul prosperity is to do exactly what it is you were created to do. This is when you enter into perfect peace, because then and only then will your soul prosper.

"The Blest Today"

Observe the successes of your predecessors. You'll see that you share many common threads. I can remember when I decided to switch my major in college from Business to English. I can still hear the messages relayed by the English Department through my coach telling me that I wasn't going to make it as an English major. I remember sitting in my coach's office and his telling me, "They just don't think you'll make it through the upper-level courses." I had a decision to make: accept their opinion and let it become my reality, or go with what I knew in my heart concerning my abilities as a writer. I walked out on the bill they set on my table concerning me as a writer. They can now pay it at any major bookstore.

It helped me to be able to refer to best-selling author Bishop T. D. Jakes when he told his stories of teachers not believing in his writing abilities. This played a major role in my decision to pursue a major in English.

If you really expect others to see in yourself what you know regarding your limitless possibilities, get ready for an uphill climb with no traction!

And you know what? I have a funny suspicion that one day, I will join Bishop Jakes on that best-seller list! Find hope through your predecessors, and you'll see. "The blest today is as completely so, As who began a thousand years ago."

—>•<—

Talent and Grace

One thing I've learned in the game of basketball is that talent is not necessarily equivalent to grace. Grace is when you actually experience success in the realm of your dream pursuit. There are players in the NBA who were obviously born to play the game—that is, the LeBrons and Kobes of the world. Then there are others at whom you look, and say, "There's got to be a player overseas who is bigger, stronger, and more athletic who could definitely get the job done better."

People miss out on their dreams because they aren't justified by their talent. God doesn't always give you the talent. That's why His grace is sufficient for all things, including your deficiencies in talent. If your heart is telling you to go in a certain direction, do it! Your heart's desires represent God's desired end. He'll get you there if you set your dreams in motion. You'll undoubtedly bypass people who are more qualified, simply because *you* have the grace to do it. We've all been bypassed by people who aren't as talented or qualified. They simply have the grace. Don't find your talent— find your grace. Hold fast to it, and let it walk you to the doorstep of your best life possible!

Ambassadors of Christ

One day as I was riding up Massachusetts Avenue in Washington, D.C., I noticed the different embassies. Each one had an architecture that resembled that of the country it represented. In essence, these ambassadors are in D.C., but they're not of D.C. They reside there, but are there to perform the tasks required of them by the country that they were sent to represent.

Your dream represents your designed space within the universe. The Success Manual says, "We are in the world, but not of the world." Your dream is your best possible output in this universe and your greatest gift to the world. You must realize that your dream doesn't respect the governing rules of society that justify your not having what it takes to actualize your dream. Your dream is subject to the laws of your Creator, who gave that dream instructions to thrive in spite of limitations placed upon you by society.

If a blade of grass can penetrate an insurmountable obstacle such as concrete, don't you think your dream has the same capability? That blade of grass does nothing more than adhere to the instructions of its Creator and keeps growing until it defeats every seemingly impossible barrier in its path.

In order to be the gift to this world that you are, you must step out of the world around you and enter into the universe to find out who your Creator says you are.

Your dream is a first-class ticket out of the land of conformity, with a destination to your best life possible!

Your Creator orchestrates the events within the universe. Your dream will separate you from the rest of the pack and be a testament to the world of your Creator in heaven.

In essence, Ambassadors do not occupy space to conform to the governing norms, they represent their countries and that's it! You are the Lord's Prayer manifested: "Thy Kingdom Come, Thy Will be done on Earth as it is in heaven." With the impossible odds you overcame upon your arrival to Earth, you must not just be a representative of the Kingdom, but rather a high-ranking official as all ambassadors are. You are a perfect extension of your Creator, dispatched from heaven carrying with you a covenant, an unbreakable promise. This promise will enable you to bring a facet of heaven to Earth if you connect with your true, supernatural self. Embrace your true essence as an ambassador of the Kingdom of Heaven, and do away with the ego-dominated thoughts that encompass this natural realm. Occupy your designed space proudly with the knowledge that the King had enough faith in you for you to be sent as His representative!

I recently arrived back from a Tony Robbins conference. He said something that I'll remember forever, "Being good or great isn't good enough anymore. This is the most competitive era in history. There are good and great employees being laid off every day because someone can do that job in an outstanding manner. In order to leave your mark you must be outstanding." If your dream is an extension of the only infallible existence there is, it has to be the most assured avenue for you to be outstanding. The box that houses the majority of society is more than overcrowded. Your future is outside of society's box. When you make it out, you'll realize that sound you heard while inside was dirt being shoveled on top of it!

In order to live a remotely comfortable life in our society, you must put your best foot forward. Just fill in the steps of the footprints that are laid before you. Follow the ready-made path of your dream to your best life possible!

You Have the Tools

Thoughts of inadequacy
Plague internal dialogue
Do I have the courage?
Do I possess the resolve?

To actualize my dream
So far out there it seems
Capable to fulfill it
Before creation you've been deemed

You have the tools
And they're perfectly measured
To your assignment here on earth
Even the storms you must weather

His time a moment
Yes, this is where dreams are made
When met with adequate preparation
Your destiny's road is now paved

Capture life's moments

They point you to your sphere

As Alexander Pope says

What matter soon or late, or here or there

Know that your Creator's most thriving business

Is that of restoration

So if there's breath in your body

Your sphere of perfection is patiently waiting

Notes and Insights

Notes and Insights

PROVIDENCE AWAITS YOU

WHEN YOU COMMIT, GOD COMMITS. LES BROWN

Providence is a supernatural endowment from your Creator that takes you from where you currently are to His designed end for you. It occurs on two fronts: internally and externally. It is set in motion the minute you commit to the dream that is in your heart. It is such a precious endowment that it in no way can be set in motion until you are fully committed to pursuing your dreams.

As human beings, our minds are too feeble to orchestrate the necessary events to get us from where we are to our designed end. But, strangely enough, when you make a commitment and begin taking steps in the direction of your dreams, you'll constantly find yourself in situations so pivotal to the fulfillment of your dreams that you'll know it resulted from divine orchestration. Being in the right place at the right time will become commonplace as your dreams unfold right in front of your eyes.

So many instances of providence have been enacted in my life that I don't know where to begin to tell you about them. One of the most recent occurred right after I graduated from college. A speaker from Texas called me and extended to me an invitation to come see him speak in New York. Since I was fresh out of college, I gladly accepted the opportunity to be in the presence of one of the industry's brightest young stars.

I arrived at the hotel where he was speaking and met a young lady who was also there to see him. We engaged in a little conversation while waiting for the event to begin. I let her know that I was a recent college graduate with aspirations of becoming a motivational speaker. She informed me that she owned a business. Out of nowhere, she said, "Are you familiar with Tony Robbins?" I told her I was. She replied, "I have a ticket to his seminar in Denver, Colorado. I've been trying to give this thing to my friends and none of them seem to want it. Maybe this isn't chance. I believe we met so I can give you this ticket."

All of her friends were business owners; I couldn't understand why they wouldn't want to attend a Tony Robbins conference. He practically only needs to make eye contact with you and your business productivity quadruples. Needless to say, I was in Denver a month later, at the feet of the most influential speaker in the world. It's as if I just walked into the situation. I didn't have to pay a dime! The universe makes allowances for people who live life on purpose.

It's Not Up to You

People will never see providence enacted in their lives if they believe it is their responsibility to bring their dreams to pass. Self-reliance chokes out dreams every day. The human mind is incapable of orchestrating the necessary events to get you from where you currently are to your designed end. But, when you make a total commitment to pursue the dream in your heart, you've enabled your Creator to enact supernatural providence on your behalf. The Creator does

The Universe Is Inviting You In: Your Best Life Possible Awaits You

not enact providence in the lives of people who aren't fully persuaded to pursue their dreams!

Notice that I used the word supernatural. Providence is what takes you out of the world around you and walks you to your space within the universe. Seeing how your Creator orchestrates events within the universe, your commitment allows Him to eradicate every governing law of our society and supernaturally place you at your intended end. If you've ever wondered how to walk on water, just set your dreams in motion and watch as your feet go where most people's heads are. Keep your eyes focused on your vision! Don't look down, or else you run the risk of sinking.

Faith is the factor that allows us to live life in the universe's graces. Because we're ever-evolving beings, a greater task awaits us at every stop along life's journey. There's a new opportunity to be stretched and to exhibit more of our God-given characteristics. As the severity of every task increases, there's more of a need to lose yourself and your way of thinking, and rely solely on your Creator and His orchestration of events to keep you afloat when the issues of life present themselves to you. There's a struggle at every level that will make you either stay in the Creator's graces through faith in Him, or go back to a life of conformity. In essence, there's water you must walk on at every level in life!

I believe the most illustrative instance of this in the Success Manual is when Peter walked on water. The reality is that Peter accomplished an impossible feat by walking on water. He just dared to believe that it was possible. When you step out of society's boat and step on top of that water, there's only one way to stay afloat, and that's to keep your eyes focused on what your Creator has told you in your heart concerning His capability to keep you afloat.

The problems of life await you when you decide to pursue your dreams. But remember, the struggle is a prelude to the victory. The struggle will take you to a place where it's sink or levitate. You must levitate above every negative opinion, every negative thought, and every obstacle that the universe sets in your path. The only hope of pulling this off is to keep your eyes squarely on your Creator. Develop an absolute vision of your dream in motion and perform your own magical David Blaine (renowned magician) rendition as you levitate above the issues of life! It's no coincidence that the Success Manual states, "Where there is no vision the people perish." The issues of life will place you in a perishing state if your vision doesn't remain intact on your way to dry land!

<hr />

The Internal

I can remember when I made the commitment to become a motivational speaker. It was something that other people had been urging me to do for quite some time. But I simply had to buy into the fact that the person people saw in the previews of my movie was me.

The summer before my sophomore year at college, I was at a basketball camp working for the Hall of Fame coach Morgan Wootten. All of the counselors had to speak encouraging words to the campers at week's end. I stepped forward naturally and just said what it was in my heart to say: "Don't let anyone's opinion concerning your abilities deter you from your dreams. You have to believe in yourself, because at times no one else will." It was a pretty simple statement, at least I thought it was until one of my fellow counselors pulled me aside and let me know otherwise. He was a funny guy—24/7 comedy. I rarely saw him in a serious mode. But on this day, he told me, with an earnest expression, "The way you spoke to those kids, that's a gift. Don't keep that to yourself! You have to share that gift!" He yanked me to the side and almost shook me up, but the vivid depiction of a scene from my movie was so evident, it drove him to take those measures.

Once you buy into the fact that it's the real you people are constantly bringing to your attention, then providence can be enacted on your behalf. A year later, after that camp counselor spoke those words into my life, and after that pivotal speech class in the spring of my sophomore year when my classmates encouraged me, I answered the call of motivational speaking. Many thoughts went through my head, such as, "I'm only nineteen, what do I know about motivational speaking?" But for so many people to constantly bring my gift to my attention, I knew there had to be some truth to it. So one day I just believed it, and I got a firsthand glimpse of supernatural providence. This was the beginning of the rest of my life.

I said, "OK, if this is the route you want me to take, God, then, not as I wilt, but as Thou wilt."

You can say you're going to become something, but to commit to being that something is speaking life into your words.

Since that day, I've been getting direct downloads from heaven. I would hear success phrases in my mind constantly, during tests, while I was asleep, anywhere you can imagine. The voice was never turned off or tuned out. I knew it wasn't me, but the result of providential forces made manifest in my internal dialogue.

From that point on, I've truly been in the spirit. Since I made a true commitment, I've had the overwhelming urge to see people living life at its optimum in every facet. There have been many obstacles I've encountered to get to this point, just as you'll face stumbling blocks in the pursuit of your dreams. Always remember that these obstacles are strategically conditioning your mind to function at the level at which your dream will require of you.

The universe does not set obstacles before you that you aren't equipped to handle. You've had the keys to overcome them even before the world was spoken into existence.

If you can maintain total reliance on God throughout your dream pursuit and in life in general, the responsibility is on Him to get you where your designed end is. This is when you've given Him permission to keep providential forces enacted in your life. Providence allows you to defy norms and do the impossible!

———•◦•———

Your Ways!

God has given us all the ability to do the impossible. Your awareness of this ability is contingent upon what has territory inside of you. Life and success are a fight for territory. It's your God-given nature battling against your ways. "Ways" are deeply imbedded habits that are detrimental to your achieving success. The vivid depiction of you gracing the stage of your destiny is your God-given nature. Your ways are the thoughts and habits that choke out those dreams. If you can keep your mind formulated in such a way that your true nature has more territory than your ways, then you've braced yourself to do the impossible in all facets of life. Believe me, fulfilling a dream and seeing it through until the end is the impossible.

The more territory that your true nature has inside of you, the more success you'll experience in life. Your ways are real! They can oftentimes be traced back to your family's lineage. I'm here to tell you that your parents and their way of doing things that you see in yourself are not the overriding factors for your success. Your parents are just the vehicle your Creator chose to bring you into this earthly realm. Your dream adheres to your Creator's instructions to thrive, and nothing else!

You may ask, "How do I defeat my ways?" This is a life-changing question. You simply stay the course! Everyone can see themselves operating in the arena of their dream before they set it in motion. As you get on the course to actualizing your dreams, the depictions of your dream become more realistic. When you see that they are more tangible, in a sense, then there's more pain associated with not achieving them. If the pain of your not achieving your dreams out-weighs your desire to continue on in your ways, you're taking steps in the direction of your dreams. When there's pain associated with your not achieving your dreams, then true change is being set in motion. You know deep down that the further you go on the path toward your dreams, the more of your ways have to die. This is how you defeat your ways and give yourself a fighting chance to achieve your dreams: STAY THE COURSE!

⸺►◄⸺

The Success Perspective

In dealing with some clients, I've realized that the victim mentality is real. I can tell them something, and there's a "but" this or "but" that in response. A huge component of your ways is based on the victim mentality. Your limitless possibilities are staring you right in the face, yet there's a "*but* this thing is so hard", "*but* there's so much opposition", "*but* you've been this way for years." "Buts" are nothing more than the issues of life everyone has to deal with. There's always a "but" present as to why you haven't achieved your dreams.

There's a reason that your butt is behind you as you face the mirror each morning. Every morning when you stand in front of that mirror, your Creator sees you with the ability to be everything He's predestined you to be, and to have the impact on this world that only YOU can have. His only desire is that you see yourself from His perspective. When it's ingrained in your heart and mind that it's not too early or too late to achieve your dreams, and that you're more than capable, this is when you've adopted the success perspective. The evidence that it's not too late is that you still have breath in your body.

Every breath you take is your Creator telling you there's still an assignment for you to complete.

The victim mentality will always keep you in a regressing state. Take charge of your life and buy into what your Creator knows concerning your limitless possibilities! Maintain the winning perspective to keep providential forces moving on your behalf. The choice is yours: either make moves on life, or life will undoubtedly make moves on you!

—————⇒•◦•⇐—————

Providence Awaits You

Providence awaits you
To buy into its plan
A best-selling author
I believe I'm that man

As I began to think this way
An orchestration of events
Was effortlessly set under way

Things I cannot explain
Seem to find their way to me
My first solo book
At the age of twenty-three

I did not know
How I would fill its pages
Until providence tapped me into
Its wisdom that transcends ages

Being in the right place
Seems to be the norm
With people telling me
I'm evolving into divine form

I'm not saying this to impress you
Nor to boast or brag
But to providential forces
I can accredit everything I have

If you would just believe
The provisions are on your path
Providence will give you her measure
From her unending bag

Providence awaits you
This is not some catchy phrase
O providence I thank you
For giving me every word that graces each page

Notes and Insights

Notes and Insights

INCLINE YOUR EARS TO
THE VOICE OF THE UNIVERSE

ABUNDANCE IS NOT SOMETHING WE ACQUIRE. IT'S SOMETHING WE TUNE INTO. DR. WAYNE DYER

The universe is always giving you overwhelming signs that point you in the direction of your space within it. The main one is that dream inside you that just won't go away despite circumstances that should have eradicated it by now. Others include those people who are constantly bringing your effortless gifts to your attention, with phrases such as "You are really good at this," or "You would make an excellent——!" The universe is constantly placing you in situations that will enable you to gain an awareness of your true self if your ear is inclined to its whispers.

The Number-One Objective

The number-one objective for our creation is that we occupy our space within this universe. Your dream represents your space. Your dream will thrive like nothing you've ever experienced in your life. Everyone receives the universe's invitations, but it's those people who accept it who rise to the forefront in life. People constantly bringing your effortless gifts to your attention are by no means a coincidence. This is God's attempt to show you the real you through an anonymous tip!

You will see vivid depictions of your movie before you ever know it's in theaters. When you accept the role, the cast begins to come together. Everything you need for your movie to become a hit suddenly finds its way to you in an effortless manner.

I gained an awareness of the effortless gifts and their pivotal roles in our self-actualization one day when I was in college. I was in my room watching a commercial featuring Jay-Z, the multi-Platinum-selling artist. He was being fitted for a custom-made suit and he asked the tailor if he'd ever purchased a Jay-Z album. The tailor replied with yes. Jay-Z then began to tell him how he had discovered that rap was his destiny. He said something like, "I used to beat on the tables in my mother's house and rhyme. People would always tell me I was good at it and that it was a gift. I did it so effortlessly that I took it for granted." Judging by his success, he must have discovered his gift.

There I was in my room, watching TV, and suddenly the idea of effortless gifts just made sense. I heard a voice say, "The effortless gifts that define your true identity are apparent to others before you're made aware of them." Don't think I'm crazy, but I do hear things like this in my head all day long. I'm the message that I bring. Once you truly align yourself with the Creator's plan for your life, He begins to think for you in the arena of your dream, and your genius is born.

I was out in Washington, D.C. not long ago, and I saw a musician playing at a small venue. When he was finished, one of his buddies pulled him to the side (sound familiar?) and told him he had what it took to become a great guitarist. His buddy saw a vivid depiction from his movie, so much so that he went into detail with the guy on how to get the ball rolling toward him playing professionally. This wasn't just another opinion, this was the real deal! The guy nonchalantly played it off and barely even entertained the idea of what his buddy was telling him. He then walked out of the establishment. This made me feel uneasy, because I could see the universe's play unfolding right in front of me. Who knows, that could have been the first day of the rest of that guy's life, but it's the effortless gifts that we take for granted.

You have to take into consideration the signs that the universe is giving you on a daily basis. Considering that we're ever-evolving beings, there's always a sign pointing you in the direction of your next step. It's the inclined eye that recognizes it! Don't make the mistake of looking too deeply into things—true signs are overwhelming and undeniable.

It's like when I was back at college, when I started off thinking I was going to be an NBA basketball player. I took that speech class and presented a speech that had a real impact on my classmates, who told me I should be a motivational speaker. That was something I had never thought about before.

It didn't end there. When I told my mother about what had occurred in the classroom that day, she said, "That's funny, someone asked me what you're going to be when you graduated, and I blurted out, 'He's going to be a motivational speaker!'" She had no idea where it came from, she just said it.

Just when I thought it was finished, I was home for spring break at a church service. My pastor called me up to the front and said, "People are out there waiting for you to speak success to them. Learn to be a coach. Your success is in obeying God." He had just got a spiritual prompting to speak these words into my life.

What's remarkable is that these three separate incidents occurred within a two-week span. When I say true signs are overwhelming and undeniable, that's exactly what I mean! There was no need to look deep into what these people were saying, rather I needed to look deep inside of myself. Man, was I at a crossroads!

➤•◆•◄

The Crossroads

The similar nature of these events made me take a look at my life and the direction it was headed. I had been clinging to this dream since I was young, to become a great NBA player. I was at a university where this could very well happen. The game of basketball is what I loved with my heart and soul. Motivational speaking? Well, I didn't know the first thing about it. I could either accept motivational speaking as my very reason for existence, or deny what the universe was screaming in my ear.

I had arrived at a place internally, where I knew in my heart that motivational speaking was the path I was supposed to take with my life. I said goodbye to *my* plan and submitted to *the plan* that God had manufactured for my life. This is my message to the world! If you want to live life at its absolute optimum, then you must remove all ceilings from your life and submit to your God-given destiny. You might say, "How do you know what your destiny is?" This is one of life's number one questions, and the strategies presented to you on these pages are my humble attempt to enable you to gain an awareness of what your IT in life truly is.

You may have the signs right there in front of you, but you just don't know how you will ever become what the universe is showing you that you already are. Believe me, I was nineteen years old when I knew in my heart that the NBA wasn't it. It hurt, but I knew that if the only infallible existence there is had created a tailor-made path to my good life, then I should take His route. I initially didn't want to go

God's route, but when reading the Success Manual, I found I was in good company.

Jesus Christ, the greatest man to have ever walked the Earth, found Himself in a similar position. He knew His fate was to die at the cross, but He asked God, "If it be possible, let this cup pass me by." But He then said the most life-altering and overlooked words in the Bible, "Not as I wilt, but as *Thou* wilt." Some of your destinies are staring you right in the face, but deep-seated feelings of inadequacy are keeping you from taking steps in the direction of it. Just say, "Nevertheless," and submit. This is the path that will solidify a legacy that endures through the ages, and walks you to the doorstep of your best life possible!

The Uncut Diamond Within

I believe that emergence is the most overlooked factor when discovering one's true self. I can remember the last conversation I had with my coach before he offered me a scholarship. I told him that I believed that I was an uncut diamond, and that with the right coaching I could shine and be marketable. I believed I had the tools to become great in the game of basketball, but I knew they would have to be cultivated through coaching. I figured I'd emerge into a great basketball player. So I went to college with the dream of becoming an NBA player.

As I mentioned before, dreams or desires don't just appear in your heart. They have a purpose behind them and are designed by the Creator to be pursued for an outcome only He knows of. Dreams truly are either your IT in life, or they're meant to put you in the vicinity of your true IT. You are like an uncut diamond at the beginning of every endeavor in life. There is a truth that awaits you at the completion of every endeavor that life sets before you. This truth can be gauged through the capacity in which you emerge throughout your dream pursuit. Emergence is the Creator's attempt to introduce you to the true you and show you your IT.

You have seen in my story how I was emerging into a motivational speaker in the midst of my hoop dreams. My diamond was being cut, not the way I had conceived that it would, but rather in the fashion it was designed to. You can't truly be disappointed when things don't go the way you envisioned at the onset of your dream pursuit. If you just see it through until the end, your true identity as a person will become clear to you. I don't care how difficult the circumstances are that surround your dream, you must be willing to go to that dark corner in which everything is happening contrary to the way you had imagined it; this is the time and space where your true identity emerges and becomes clear to you. Yes, go to the abyss with your dreams!

It's a dark corner when your coach takes you, a full-scholarship athlete, to a road game and makes you sit in the stands and tape the game. It's a dark corner when you're told that you can't dress for a game because a pair of shorts is missing and we think our walk-ons are more suited to play than you. It's in the abyss where your true genius, brilliance, and greatness emerges. This is the time when God showed me life's processes through the game of basketball. This is the time when I should have quit by all means, and people wouldn't have been upset with me. What can I say—I went on to get my first book contract at the age of twenty-two. The victory that awaited me on the other side of the struggle exemplified the definition of a light affliction.

The only meaningful element at the end of a dream pursuit really is truth—not success or failure. You're constantly evolving and emerging during your dream pursuit. That's why I can say with confidence that emergence represents the truth of who you are. Emergence is your Creator telling you, "This is what I put you here to do."

Thinking back to high school, my dream was to become a Division I basketball player. It didn't look like it was going to happen until my senior season, when I emerged into the kind of player who could receive a full athletic scholarship. The perception of myself that I had when I entered high school regarding what I would become was actually the truth. Dreams that facilitate success in the arena in which they place you are truth. During the process of dream pursuit, just look at how you're emerging and find truth. That dream may be your IT or it may be meant to put you in the vicinity of your TRUE IT! Your Creator knows exactly how your diamond needs to be cut to bring Him that sparkle. Just set your dreams in motion and watch the Sculptor go to work!

$$\longrightarrow\!\!\bullet\!\!\longleftarrow$$

Incline Your Ears

It's the inclined ear
Which hears the universe's voice
A selection which to you
May not be your first choice

If I had it my way
I'd be in the NBA
But this is contrary to that whisper
And what its contents did say

"You should be a motivational speaker"
At every turn I seemed to hear
It is the place that was established
Opposite of what I held so dear

But if this is the path
You'd like for me to take
Then nevertheless
For it is your glory that is at stake

Oftentimes your destiny

Is staring right at you

Through your effortless gifts

Universal light glares on you

If you would just believe

They're talking about you

When you impact others

With that thing that you do

Destiny is difficult to decipher

Without an inclined ear

That voice of your dream's possibilities

To it, draw near

You'll see the universe

Will reveal its ready-made path

Your best life possible

Its grandeur will make you gasp

Notes and Insights

The Universe Is Inviting You In: Your Best Life Possible Awaits You

PRECISION LIVING

A CLEAR-CUT VISION AND THE WHEREWITHAL TO SEE IT TO COMPLETION
SERVE AS A LIFE PRESERVER TO THE SEA OF MEDIOCRITY.   MATTHEW C. HORNE

Keeping your eye squarely on your vision in life places everything in its proper perspective. You might have your ways that you've struggled with for years. When you stay on course toward your dreams, that now tangible dream which was once so far out there will properly align everything in your life. The further you go toward your dreams, the more they will consume you. When you're consumed by a dream it will make decisions for you, intelligent ones. The most intelligent decisions you could ever make are from the standpoint of your vision. Ask yourself, "Is this helping me get closer to, or is it taking me further away from, my vision?"

Successful people live life with precision simply because their vision does their thinking for them.

You must totally immerse yourself in your vision so that it takes territory inside of you and begins to make every decision for you. The more you immerse yourself in your vision, the more territory it takes inside of you. As your vision takes more territory, your ability to live life with precision is drastically improved. The more precise your life becomes, the easier it is to make quality decisions that will accelerate the path toward your destiny. Vision, when it consumes you, will rearrange every facet of your life so that it is conducive to your achieving your dreams. Believe me, this is what you want! When every facet of your life is geared toward your achieving your dreams, that is when you truly live life with precision.

The further you go into life, the more is at stake, and therefore the need for precision living becomes more critical with every passing year. It's important that you take steps in the direction of your dreams every day, week, month, and year. Even in the midst of pursuing your dreams, you must maintain an unbreakable focus on achieving them so that the issues of this world don't choke them out. The further you go in the direction of your dreams, the greater the obstacles that appear in your path.

———➤◦◄———

Your Dream's Momentum

When you get to the point in life when your dream begins to think for you, and it's the determining factor for your every decision, your dream will be accompanied with a renewed momentum. Dr. Maya Angelou says, "Most people only go so far in life, and then they park." When your dream has precedence and the momentum that fuels it, anything that is detrimental to your achieving that dream must be immediately dealt with. This is what I mean when I talk about having your dream make intelligent decisions for you. There are factors in every one of our lives that make us park at times. Relationships that are dead, associations that are toxic to our growth, and fear that paralyzes us are a few of the factors that keep us parked in life.

When you immerse yourself in your dream and it begins to gain momentum, you can do away with anything that is detrimental to your achieving that dream in a heartbeat! Your dream is accompanied by a spiritual energy that creates a noticeable momentum. Anything that interferes with this momentum is easily identifiable, because you'll be expending your energy elsewhere. If something has taken your momentum, just take inventory and you will easily identify the culprit. Your dream, when it thinks for you, is the epitome of intelligent decision-making and precision living.

Your dream is your treasure, and that which you treasure most is what you'll give your energy to. The Success Manual says "Guard your heart with all diligence, because out of it flows the issues of life." The "issues" are the atmosphere you create for your life, which is a by-product of where you're expending the most energy. When your dream spews out of your heart as a result of it consuming you, it will create the atmosphere around you necessary to see your dream through to completion. As human beings, we possess the power to create our own atmosphere, but when your dream is doing your thinking, your dream creates its own atmosphere and guards it with diligence because it is the issue you've been created for, and your every reason for existence. Success is an intrinsic matter. This is a way to go inside yourself and create the environment necessary to achieve your dream. Don't give your treasure to what society or "security" says you ought to be; give your treasure to your heart's desires, and you'll ensure the path to your best life possible!

People with no vision allow anything into their environment, because nothing has consumed them except simply existing and conforming to societal norms.

We are hard-wired as human beings to stay the course toward the vision that has consumed us.

Your vision is the Kingdom of God inside of you. Our life's quest is to return to the Kingdom of God while still on Earth—to manifest

God's will on Earth as it has been in heaven for the ages. God can't simply come to Earth and get His will done Himself. So He dispensed each and every one of us to Earth, accompanied with an assignment that only we can complete, and set us on the path we call life in the hope that we'll listen to the inner voice of our true selves—that voice telling us our dreams are possible. Yes, that voice telling you that nothing can interfere with the divine plan for your life if you simply set it in motion.

Your Creator placed an extension of Himself in you, which has no regard for any of the world's governing stipulations that validate your ability to achieve your God-given assignment. Those conversations you hear inside yourself regarding your limitless possibilities are nothing more than your Creator talking with the extension of Him that He's placed inside of you. If success has eluded you, perhaps you should begin eavesdropping on these conversations. The minute you believe the person they are talking about is you, is the minute you've arrived at the doorstep of your best life possible!

You Were Created with a Price

Your life is not your own. This is why the Success Manual states that we are bought with a price. Each and every one of us has a price on our head. This price is the covenant that God made with us by dispatching us from the heavenly realm to the Earth to carry out a divine plan that will bring Him glory. A covenant is an unbreakable bond or promise. Our destinies had to be delivered to us in the form of a covenant, because our Creator knew that no good thing dwells in this fallible Earth suit that houses the perfect extension of Himself. In essence, we have the ability to become everything we've been fore-ordained to be with no interference from any opposition we'll face, which is mainly ourselves on the quest to fulfill the divine covenant that was spoken over us before creation, and which more often than not manifests itself in the form of a dream that harasses us until we conform. View yourself as a walking, talking covenant and nothing will ever stop you from becoming everything your heart says you are!

Get Thee Out of Thy Country

The obstacles increase in size as you are nearing your victory, that actualization of what you've been working so hard to achieve. The game is almost won and you're nearing your finish line. At every level of basketball I've ever participated in, I can remember a play called "1–4." This is an isolation play that is used when an offensive player has a mismatch against his defender, and is thought to be able to score on him at will. In late-game situations with the score close, you want the ball in the hands of your best player. This offers the most assured chance there is to solidify a victory. All of the players are spread out on the court in a manner in which the best player has enough room to take on his defender one-on-one and score the basket with limited interference from his teammates' defenders.

A time will come in your dream pursuit when you know you're close to scoring that basket. You've been through the entire game of pursuing your dreams, and you feel the pressures associated with the fourth quarter. This is when you separate yourself as best as you can from any hindering force that could keep you from achieving your dreams. Put the ball in the hands of your best possible player: your dream! Believe me, at this point you've got to battle internal as well as external hindering forces that are detrimental to achieving your dream. Focus squarely on achieving your dream: it has instructions to score every time, and is not subject to any strategies of opposing forces. If you keep the ball in the hands of your dream when the end is nearing, the Coach of all coaches will see to it that your dream emerges triumphant!

Everyone knows the hindering forces that are in place to choke out your respective dreams. When I say, "Get thee out of thy country," this isn't in terms of logistics, it's an attempt to remove you from your personal comfort zones.

You have to keep attacking when you're nearing that finish line. I remember that time at the end of my senior season in college, when my coach was relieved of his head coaching duties. The athletic director met with our entire team and told us of his decision to let my coach go. Of the reasons that were given, one stands out the most, "There were too many late-game situations when you guys had the lead and it slipped away. You guys would hold the ball instead of attacking. It's as if you played not to lose instead of playing to win."

When you find yourself in that late-game situation in pursuing your dreams, you must keep attacking in spite of increased pressure from any opposition. Remember, you're either going forward or backward at all times in your life. Stagnation is an illusion. If you wait until the clock has almost expired before you decide to make your move, you'll undoubtedly take a bad shot.

You know the defense is coming. Make moves on it. You know those people who are vision blockers; get away from them! Surround yourself with vision builders who see eye-to-eye with what you know in your heart regarding the possibilities of your dream. You know those ways that you have that aren't conducive to the actualization of your dream; don't put yourself in surroundings that cater to your ways; instead, place yourself in an environment that is beneficial to your achieving that dream. Make moves on the defense before you find yourself in a late-game situation with your dream, and you're playing on your heels! Your success is there for the taking. Position yourself to make precise moves that keep you one step ahead of your dream's opposition. Keep the ball in the hands of your dream and ATTACK!

Life's Recurrent Cycle

The Bible says, "Wisdom is the principal thing." It's the principal thing that needs to be in order to live a life of precision. Life is nothing more than a series of recurrences. The same series of events present themselves to you over and over again. The only difference between these events is that there's less time left with each recurrence, therefore reinforcing the need to live with precision. In essence, you can't continue to make the same mistakes over and over again and expect to arrive at your destiny.

At every difficult situation that you overcome in life, there is new wisdom at your disposal. Precision comes into play when you can apply the knowledge from a previous situation when a similar one arises, and use it to make an intelligent decision regarding the new situation. Knowledge applied is wisdom. Wisdom is what enables people to continue to soar to unseen heights in life.

Life has given you a knowledge account that suits you perfectly.

Extract knowledge from your account and let it create principal in your life's bank.

Precision Living

The further you go in life
The more is at stake
Truthfully speaking
The end is more near
With every breath that you take

Mistakes cannot be duplicated
Life must be lived with precision
Your vision must be your guide
For every decision

Is this getting me closer to
Or is this taking me away
From the stage of my destiny
I will occupy one day

Purpose protects you
From mundane routine
As you stay the course
Vivid depictions are now seen

That dream

Which seemed so far away

Vivid depictions of it entrusted you

As the course you did stay

Don't worry

Your shortcomings will never interfere with fate

As your vision consumes you

With destiny you have a date

With every facet of your life

Now perfectly aligned

God-given nature consuming you

You've entered the divine

Notes and Insights

The Universe Is Inviting You In: Your Best Life Possible Awaits You

CONCLUSION

It is my desire that the words on these pages have not left you motivated, but inspired. I've arrived at the conclusion that motivation doesn't last. You can be motivated to do anything; you can be inspired to do just one thing: carry out THE PLAN for your life. I hope that after reading this book, you have an in-spirit consciousness of the person God intended for you to be. Inspiration is nothing more than being in spirit. The spiritual realm is where your destiny is housed. A constant connection with your dream and its possibilities will always keep you connected to the supernatural and enable you to live a divine life, and do away with ego-based realities concerning your dream.

My reasoning for saying that motivation doesn't last is that motivation is an end to a natural means. Anything that is based in this natural realm has an end. Your destiny, which is a spiritual matter, dwells in an infinite realm, and has an accompanying energy that will carry you across the finish line every time. Spiritual energy is what you tap into when you truly connect to the supernatural plan for your life. This is the energy that accompanies every God-inspired dream with an assignment to manifest the divine plan for your life that was spoken before creation. This energy knows nothing of shortage or lack. All it knows is the plan that it is assigned to, and it won't leave you until the job is done!

It's no wonder people walk away from things they've started. I've heard it over and over again, "I just didn't have the motivation to finish." Sustained energy is relegated according to truth; relegated to your destiny! That's why I implore you to pursue your God-given dream! There is a truth and provision that transcends time and space. It will be apparent to you upon the completion of your dream. When you cross the finish line, you will relish the phrase, "Impossible is nothing." Yes, I do carry the title of motivational speaker, but it is my desire—at the end of every speech I give, article I write, or book I publish—to leave you with an in-spirit consciousness and a knowing that your dream is possible.

Just Take a Risk

During my junior year of college I heard the most influential sermon of my life. I've heard many, but no message still permeates my way of thinking like this one does. The lesson was about taking risks. The preacher began to tell a story about a man who interviewed a number of elderly people while they were on their deathbeds. The question at hand was, "If you could have done anything different with your life, what would you have done?" The three most consistent answers were as follows: "I would have communed with God more," "I would have taken more risks," and "I would have left something that lived on beyond me [a legacy]." I thought to myself, *wow*, what a profound story! It wasn't until two years later that I got the full understanding of how these answers are interrelated.

If you commune with God, or develop a relationship with Him, He will, without question, reveal His plan for your life to you. This plan will always go against your logical thinking and require you to see past the realm of your possibilities, and rely on His infinite possibilities. This is the risk the preacher talked about. If you take the risk and set your dreams in motion, you'll have a legacy that is solidified for the ages! You'll impact this world in a way only YOU can! It doesn't matter whether society views your dream as major or minor—if you see it through to completion, it will affect many people—more than you know—and live on in their hearts.

Dr. Myles Munroe says, "Long lived is not an indicator of well done." When you make your exit from this earthly realm, you want to die empty. Jesus Christ died at the age of thirty-three, but he died empty. There are people in their hundreds who have died with their dreams still inside of them. People die every day, still full of potential that has never become reality. Those diamonds that we all possess are meant to contribute to the wealth of this world, not that of the cemetery. I implore you to get out all of your dreams and desires that won't go away. Tell your Creator that you are tired of carrying your dreams inside of you, and ask Him to help you extract your dreams so that you can be the gift to this world that only He knows you are. You have brilliance, genius, and greatness that surpass anything you could ever imagine, but it takes faith to extract them from your core being.

Anything worthwhile in life involves a risk, and the corresponding faith to see that risk through to reality.

If life seems to overwhelm you at times, look no further than the Bible for your solution. It is truly the greatest Success Manual ever assembled. My reasoning for saying this is that I judge the greatness of a man by the legacy he leaves. No other legacy exists today that is greater than that of Jesus Christ, and no other legacy has permeated the ages like that of Jesus Christ. So, if you have a book by and about the greatest man to have ever walked the Earth, then technically speaking, the Bible is the greatest Success Manual ever assembled. For every natural problem there's a supernatural solution; it's called FAITH! It will conquer any of life's mountains and prove it to be a molehill.

You more than have what it takes. I hope that you can see that your Creator is constantly orchestrating the necessary events in your life, so it unfolds the way He knows it should. I don't care how grim your life circumstances may be—you are perfect. You have more favor working on your behalf than you could ever conceive. You are your Creator's chosen. He's just waiting for you to commit to that dream so you can reside in His graces and find your place within His universe. Notice I didn't say your destiny awaits you—providence awaits you. All the events necessary are there, just waiting for your total commitment in order to get that motion picture of your dream constantly playing in your head out and into the theaters!

If I could leave you with just one thought, it would be this: If you are willing to set your dreams in motion, and uncompromisingly see them through until the end, your BEST LIFE POSSIBLE awaits you!

ABOUT THE AUTHOR

MATTHEW C. HORNE, motivational speaker and author, is a native of Fort Washington, Maryland, a suburb of Washington, D.C. He is the co-author of the book *A Massive Dose of Motivation.* He is the president and CEO of Optimum Success International, a professional speaking and publishing company located in the metropolitan Washington, D.C. area.

In playing collegiate basketball for four years, Matthew received more than he bargained for. Anticipating a successful basketball career and a college degree to encompass his college experience, he discovered his passion for motivational speaking by observing life's processes through the game of basketball, and applying them to everyday life experiences. Matthew's evolution as a speaker during his college years enabled him to sign his first book contract at the age of twenty-two before he graduated from college. He now desires nothing more than to serve as the bridge that connects people to their best life possible.

The Universe Is Inviting You In: Your Best Life Possible Awaits You

QUICK ORDER FORM

Please send the following books, disks or reports. I understand that I may return any of them for a full refund—for any reason, no questions asked.

Please send more FREE information on:

_ Other Books   _ Speaking/Seminars

_ Mailing Lists   _ Consulting

Name: _____

Address: _____

City: _____ State: __ Zip: _____

Telephone: _____

Email address: _____

Sales tax
Please add 5.00% for products shipped to Maryland addresses.

Shipping by air
U.S. $4.00 for first book or disk and $2.00 for each additional product.

International
$9.00 for first book or disk; $5.00 for each additional product.

Email orders
orders@matthewchorne.com

Mail orders
Optimum Success International
P.O. Box 441328, Fort Washington, MD 20744, USA.
Telephone: 240-605-1106